The Peacetime Tempo of Air Mobility Operations: Meeting Demand and Maintaining Readiness

Brian G. Chow

T0306600

RAND | Project AIR FORCE

Prepared for the United States Air Force

Approved for public release; distribution unlimited

The research reported here was sponsored by the United States Air Force under Contract F49642-01-C-0003. Further information may be obtained from the Strategic Planning Division, Directorate of Plans, Hq USAF.

Library of Congress Cataloging-in-Publication Data

Chow, Brian G.
The peacetime tempo of air mobility operations : meeting demand and maintaining readiness / Brian G. Chow.
p. cm.
"MR-1506."
ISBN 0-8330-3262-3
1. Airmobile operations (Military science) 2. United States. Air Mobility Command. 3. Airlift, Military—United States. 4. United States. Air Force—Operational readiness. I.Title.

UG633 .C52 2003
358.4'4'0973—dc21

2002033709

Cover photo courtesy of The Boeing Company (www.boeing.com/companyoffices/gallery/images/c17/DVD-32-08.htm). Reprinted by permission.

RAND is a nonprofit institution that helps improve policy and decisionmaking through research and analysis. RAND® is a registered trademark. RAND's publications do not necessarily reflect the opinions or policies of its research sponsors.

Cover design by Barbara Angell Caslon

© Copyright 2003 RAND

All rights reserved. No part of this book may be reproduced in any form by any electronic or mechanical means (including photocopying, recording, or information storage and retrieval) without permission in writing from RAND.

Published 2003 by RAND
1700 Main Street, P.O. Box 2138, Santa Monica, CA 90407-2138
1200 South Hayes Street, Arlington, VA 22202-5050
201 North Craig Street, Suite 202, Pittsburgh, PA 15213-1516
RAND URL: http://www.rand.org/
To order RAND documents or to obtain additional information, contact Distribution Services: Telephone: (310) 451-7002; Fax: (310) 451-6915; Email: order@rand.org

PREFACE

Air mobility forces are organized, trained, and equipped to simultaneously satisfy two objectives: meet peacetime demand and maintain wartime readiness. Peacetime demands can fluctuate greatly and unexpectedly, as evidenced by the tempo of U.S. military operations in the 1990s decade. Peacetime demands, both too high and too low, can lead to problems during wartime and to longer-term problems once the air mobility forces return to peacetime operations.

RAND's Project AIR FORCE has recently completed three studies of the air mobility forces. This study assesses Air Mobility Command operations at an aggregate level to better understand the characteristics of peacetime tempo, its potential effects, and alternatives for fixing emerging problems. A related study (*Waging Peace: Addressing the Peacetime Tempo of the Mobility Air Forces*, MR-1574-AF, forthcoming) assesses the stresses that the peacetime operations tempo has imposed on air mobility forces at the unit level. Another study ("Enduring Challenge: The Impact of the Global War on Terrorism on Air Mobility Forces," forthcoming with limited distribution) examines air mobility support in Operation Noble Eagle and Operation Enduring Freedom, as well as challenges that could be faced in future operations conducted in support of the global war on terrorism. Together, these studies provide important insights into challenges faced by the air mobility forces in peacetime and war, and they identify specific problems that need to be addressed.

This report compares the peacetime tempo of air mobility operations during the Cold War with that of the post–Cold War period. It then identifies potential problems that would impede the ability of the Air Mobility Command to meet peacetime demand and maintain wartime readiness. Finally, it suggests corrective measures to alleviate the identified problems. It should be of interest to analysts, military planners, and policymakers concerned with air mobility operations in both peacetime and wartime.

Although the bulk of this research was completed just prior to the September 11, 2001 terrorist attacks, the report also assesses how post-attack activities affect air mobility operations. It finds that the new emphasis on counterterrorism does not change the author's recommended corrective measures.

This project is sponsored by the Plans and Programs Directorate of the Air Mobility Command (AMC/XP). The research was conducted in the Aerospace Force Development Program within Project AIR FORCE.

PROJECT AIR FORCE

Project AIR FORCE, a division of RAND, is the Air Force federally funded research and development center (FFRDC) for studies and analyses. It provides the Air Force with independent analyses of policy alternatives affecting the development, employment, combat readiness, and support of current and future aerospace forces. Research is performed in four programs: Aerospace Force Development; Manpower, Personnel, and Training; Resource Management; and Strategy and Doctrine.

CONTENTS

FIGURES

TABLES

SUMMARY

Although the September 11 terrorist attacks and the 2001 Quadrennial Defense Review (QDR) have led the Department of Defense (DoD) leadership to change its terms of reference for sizing and planning its force, these events have not changed the dual objectives of U.S. peacetime air mobility operations: to meet peacetime demand and to maintain wartime readiness. This study compares the peacetime tempo of air mobility operations in the Cold War (the 1980s) with that of the post–Cold War period (the 1990s)[1] and examines the factors and associated trends that can affect the Air Mobility Command's (AMC's) ability to meet these dual objectives in a cost-effective manner. Does AMC have the flexibility to generate enough flying hours for pilot training when flying demand is low? Can AMC man flying operations with the number of pilots Congress has authorized? How well does the actual ratio of copilots (CPs) to aircraft commanders (ACs) match what is authorized? Comparing peacetime operations in the 1980s with those of the 1990s, did pilots get less hands-on training during flights in the latter period? Was AMC less able to project airlift demand accurately in the latter than in the former period? Did AMC have to fly more missions with shorter advance notice? Has AMC been successful in using reimbursements from its customers to defray its operating expenses? We will first report our findings on these factors and trends and will then suggest measures to correct the problems we have identified.

The aircraft examined herein are the key AMC platforms: strategic airlifters (the C-5, C-141, and C-17), tactical airlifters (the C-130), and tankers (the KC-135 and KC-10). We used data that either appeared in AMC official documents or were provided to us by AMC offices. Although the bulk of this research was completed just prior to the September 11 attacks, we have discussed in this report how postattack activities have affected air mobility operations and have

[1]Generally, whether a year is fiscal or calendar will be made evident in this report. Where neither is specified, fiscal year is intended. The peacetime period in the 1990s does not include the Gulf War–affected years, FY 1990 and FY 1991, or 1994, a unique year in which many C-141s were grounded because of possible weep-hole cracks in their wings.

found that the new emphasis on counterterrorism does not change our recommended corrective measures.

POTENTIAL PROBLEMS IDENTIFIED

Using a number of measures to analyze the historic data over the past two decades, we found problems that have the potential to hinder AMC's ability to conduct air mobility operations in a cost-effective fashion.

Flying-Hour Shortages Occurred in FY 2000 and FY 2001 and Are Likely to Recur

During FY 2000 and FY 2001, the CPs of all airlifters and tankers encountered a flying-hour shortage because the international situation was relatively calm and there were fewer U.S. missions that called for airlift support. To combat this shortage, AMC cut back on commercial expansion buys and flew organic (AMC-owned) aircraft more frequently but with smaller loads. These measures reduced but did not eliminate the shortage during those years. During FY 2000, actual CP flying hours fell short by 13 percent, 17 percent, 21 percent, 16 percent, 1 percent, and 4 percent for the C-5, C-141, C-17, C-130, KC-135, and KC-10, respectively. Even with stronger corrective action by AMC, the shortages during FY 2001 were still 6 percent, 14 percent, 9 percent, 27 percent, 6 percent, and 24 percent, respectively.

Operation Enduring Freedom (OEF) ended the flying-hour shortage, as has been the case with all previous high-airlift-demand contingencies. When OEF ends, however, the demand will return to peacetime levels, during which shortages are likely to recur from time to time. Moreover, wartime mobility requirements continue to trend higher. For example, the Air Force recently committed to buying 60 more C-17s and will likely buy even more later. Having more aircraft requires more pilots and more flying hours for training during peacetime.

We also found that annual flying hours per aircraft for the C-5, C-141, C-130, KC-10, and KC-135 were not higher during the post–Cold War era than during the Cold War. In other words, these aircraft did not fly more in the 1990s as many thought.

The Actual Number of Copilots and Aircraft Commanders Exceeded That Authorized

Since 1986, the actual number of CPs and ACs at AMC has consistently exceeded what Congress has authorized—a trend that increased at an average rate of 1 percent per year from 1982 to 2001.

The Actual Copilot-to-Aircraft Commander Ratio Deviated from That Authorized

During the 1980s and 1990s, the actual CP/AC ratios for airlifters and tankers deviated significantly from those authorized. During 2001, the actual ratios of all four airlifters were above those authorized, while those of the two tankers continued to be well below their authorized numbers.

Less Piloting Occurred During Training

The current AMC rule for meeting training requirements credits all aircraft flying hours toward every member of an aircrew, regardless of whether a pilot is controlling the aircraft from a pilot seat or merely observing others piloting elsewhere in the aircraft. An increase in the average number of pilots per flight means that pilots are getting less actual piloting opportunity and experience.

During the 1980s and 1990s, all airlifters had an increasing number of pilots per flight. The number of pilots per C-5 flight, for example, increased an average of 2 percent per year, while that per C-141 flight rose by 3.2 percent. The C-17 showed a large upward trend of 9.6 percent per year, but the trend for this aircraft, which was newly deployed at the time, should level off as its operations mature. The C-130 showed an upward trend of 0.6 percent per year.

Deviations from the Flying Plan Increased

The actual flying hours of the C-5, C-141, and C-130 showed an increasing annual deviation[2] from the current plan, although that plan was adjusted every few months throughout each fiscal year to better match demand. By the late 1990s, these annual deviations were roughly double those of the early 1980s. A rise in short-notice flights can make the scheduling of flights and maintenance more complicated and can negatively affect pilots' quality of life.

Two other measures were used to study these deviations. In any given year, there can be months in which actual flying hours exceed those planned only a few months before. The month with the largest excess is that with the peak (monthly) greater-than-planned (GTP) flying level for the year. During the 1980s and 1990s, the C-5, C-141, and C-130 showed an increasing peak GTP flying level from one year to the next. The larger the GTP flying level, the greater the number of aircraft and personnel that must be quickly gathered together to meet the peak monthly demand of the year. The peak GTP flying level for C-5s

[2]The annual deviation is the sum of the absolute values of both positive and negative monthly deviations in a given fiscal year.

and C-141s in the late 1990s was double that of the early 1980s, while the peak level for C-130s was three times that of the previous period.

A third measure was used to estimate the length of time the actual monthly flying level had exceeded what was planned. For example, if actual monthly flying hours exceeded those planned for four months in a row, the length was considered to be four months. A longer length of time increasingly burdens the air mobility system, which must sustain the effort of gathering extra aircraft and personnel for a longer period of time. We found, however, that this length changed little during the 1980s and 1990s for any of the four airlifters, remaining at two to three months.

Engagement Missions Accounted for a Growing Share of Missions

Engagement missions such as banner operations (presidential support), humanitarian relief operations, and special assignment airlift missions (SAAMs) contain more short-notice flights than do channel missions or operation and maintenance (O&M) missions. Short-notice flights are more difficult and costly to schedule than routine, planned missions and have a more negative effect on pilots' quality of life. Engagement missions for each of the airlifters were found to account for a growing share of flying hours during the periods studied. For the C-5, these missions accounted for only 11 percent of all missions flown in 1981 but represented 68 percent by 1999. For the C-141, this share increased from 26 percent in 1981 to 38 percent in 1999, while that of the C-17 increased from 9 percent in 1995 to 46 percent by 1999. Finally, the share for the C-130 increased from 21 percent in 1981 to 40 percent in 1999.

Fewer of AMC's Flying Expenses Were Reimbursed by Customers

AMC was less able to recoup its training and operating expenses in the 1990s than in the 1980s because the reimbursable Transportation Working Capital Fund (TWCF) share of AMC's operating budget declined during that period. Specifically, TWCF constituted 70 percent of the budget in 1984, but by 1999 this figure had been reduced to 51 percent. Further, commercial air carriers took a rising proportion of the TWCF, leaving even less money for AMC; overall, commercial carriers' share rose from 23 percent in 1981 to 32 percent in 1999. This increasing commercial penetration was particularly prominent in channel cargo, AMC's favorite mission category for pilot training, where the commercial share rose from 24 percent in 1981 to 46 percent in 1999. Moreover, commercial providers continued to dominate channel passenger miles, capturing 90 percent of this business since 1981. Allowing commercial providers to assume a greater portion of airlift service during peacetime is acceptable only if AMC has the flexibility to increase and decrease its commercial buy in any particular year to accommodate its organic flying capacity and requirement.

We also found that the percentages of channel passengers riding free on both organic and AMC-chartered commercial flights continued to be significant, standing at 65 percent and 29 percent, respectively, in FY 1999. This represented a further loss of revenue to AMC.

SUGGESTED CORRECTIVE MEASURES TO DEAL WITH THE RECURRING FLYING-HOUR SHORTAGE AND REVENUE LOSS

Corrective measures should first address the most difficult problem, AMC's recurring flying-hour shortage. However, we review the measures already implemented by AMC to correct this shortage before we suggest additional ones. Once this problem of shortage is resolved, the often-associated issue of loss of revenue as well as other problems will become easier to remedy. Overall, our corrective measures are designed to be flexible so that even an excessive flying demand—which is also likely to occur from time to time—can be handled.

Offer Measures Beyond Those Taken by AMC

Since FY 2000, AMC has been taking measures to combat its flying-hour shortage. First, AMC cut $89 million from its international cargo buy during the first eleven months of FY 2001 prior to the September 11 attacks and retained more flying for its own pilots.

Second, AMC has been considering the possibility of reducing the flying-hour requirement for C-130 CPs from 29 hours to 24 or 25 hours per month and the total hours required for promotion to AC from 1000 hours to 900 hours. However, AMC needs to show how this requirement can be reduced without affecting training and qualification.

Third, AMC decided not to correct the flying-hour shortage for C-141 CPs because C-141s will soon be retired. However, this can present a problem in that C-141 CPs will be transferred to fly other aircraft such as C-17s, and their earned flying hours will count toward the requirement for promotion to AC regardless of the aircraft to which they are assigned. Thus, reducing CP flying hours will delay CPs' promotion. In any case, AMC needs to show that a flying-hour reduction will still result in adequate training and will not affect flight safety in C-141 and other aircraft types.

Fourth, during FY 2001, AMC was able to reduce but not eliminate the flying-hour shortage for the CPs of C-5s and C-17s by flying channel cargo missions more frequently and carrying less. Had AMC completely eliminated this shortage, the extra flights throughout FY 2001 would have cost it approximately $70 million, or 11 percent of the C-5 and C-17 flying-hour cost. Had AMC used the same approach to eliminate the flying-hour shortage for the CPs of its other airlifters (C-141s and C-130s) and for those of its tankers (KC-135s and KC-10s), it would have incurred an additional annual cost of $144 million for a future year that happened to have an airlift demand as low as that of FY 2001. Moreover, the shortage could worsen from time to time in the future and cost AMC even more.

Fifth, although the aircrew for many strategic airlifters (the C-5, C-141, and C-17) has consisted of two ACs and one CP, AMC encouraged wing commanders to replace the second AC with a CP on these flights. However, wing commanders often consider it risky to do so given that C-17s are still new and their CPs relatively inexperienced. Moreover, the C-17 flight crew has neither a flight engineer nor a navigator. Even for C-5s and C-141s, two ACs are considered necessary to handle flights involving complicated operations despite the fact that two flight engineers are also on board. We believe that the replacement of the second AC with a CP is a corrective measure that is both attractive and readily available and, as such, should be used whenever it does not affect flight safety and the CPs have insufficient flying hours.

Sixth, AMC has developed a new initiative, Channel Door to Door (CD2), in which it retains the option to use its airlifters for the flying segment and contracts Civil Reserve Air Fleet (CRAF) participants for the ground segment. CD2 allows AMC to fly more whenever it needs to do so to meet its pilot training requirements. CD2 commenced on October 1, 2001, and was expected to replace $10 million, or one-fifth of the buys from the Commercial Air Line of Communications (COMALOC), during FY 2002. In addition to CD2, AMC has been attempting to fold many air cargo tenders into the Military Air Line of Communications (MILALOC). While a tender is not under TWCF, a MILALOC is. Commercial international tenders account for $25 million to $30 million per year, and retaining any part of those funds through MILALOC will result in more flying hours as well as more revenue for AMC. On the other hand, CD2 and cutbacks in tenders, while beneficial and worthy of development, are insufficient to eliminate a shortage similar in size to that which appeared during FY 2000 and FY 2001.

Worse, the flying-hour shortage may become even more severe from time to time because AMC will be increasing its number of pilots. Moreover, although AMC has taken measures to alleviate the flying-hour shortage, such measures can be expensive and, even when combined, are insufficient to resolve a severe shortage. The paragraphs below suggest additional measures that can help alleviate even a severe shortage.

Further Reduce the International Cargo Buy

We suggest that the international cargo buy be further reduced when a flying-hour shortage recurs. During peacetime years in which flying-hour shortages are of magnitude similar to those that occurred in FY 2001,[3] the international cargo buy would have to be reduced by another $90 million (out of $200 million) in order to completely eliminate the shortage for the C-5 and C-17 CPs alone at the current level. AMC will have to cut to a bare minimum not only its expansion buy but also its fixed buy. We suggest that a cancellation fee be paid to the affected commercial carriers if their incentives to stay in CRAF become insufficient because of the cut. This fee arrangement would still be cheaper than flying organic aircraft more frequently but with less cargo.

Add an Organic, Dedicated Passenger-Carrying Capability

AMC needs to increase its flexibility in meeting fluctuating demand, both high and low, without sacrificing readiness. Gaining flexibility is consistent with the 2001 QDR's new "basis of defense planning from a 'threat-based' model that has dominated thinking in the past to a 'capabilities-based' model for the future."[4] Because the United States cannot predict when and how often war might occur, it is important that AMC acquire this flexibility.

The international cargo buy, which has long served as a flying-hour reservoir, might run low when a shortage recurs. AMC can double its flexibility by creating another flying-hour reservoir from the international passenger buy, which is the planeload charter on commercial aircraft. Its volume is about $350 million a year and is even larger than the international cargo buy. There is sufficient traffic for AMC to carry planeloads of passengers economically. Currently, however, AMC does not have dedicated long-range passenger carriers with which to carry passengers by the planeload.

Rather than acquire passenger aircraft, AMC would find it much cheaper to convert an airlifter or a tanker from carrying cargo to delivering passengers. The conversion set should, however, be designed to be installed and uninstalled quickly and cheaply.

AMC is already considering buying palletized seats for 34 C-17s and storing them for wartime use. It would be more cost-effective, however, for AMC to use

---

[3]Because we are interested in peacetime demand that is not driven up by high-airlift demand contingencies, we refer here to the size of demand in FY 2001, with a small adjustment of excluding the added activities for the aftermath of September 11 attacks during September.

[4]See *Quadrennial Defense Review Report*, Washington, D.C.: U.S. Department of Defense, September 30, 2001, p. iv.

these seats during peacetime to generate some needed flying hours as well. A conversion set would cost roughly $300,000 per C-17, and eliminating the flying hour shortage experienced in FY 2001 and possibly recurring in the future for C-17 CPs would require a dozen C-17s carrying passengers. The capital outlay for a dozen C-17 conversion sets would be only $3.6 million. Moreover, if AMC decided to buy those palletized seats for 34 C-17s for other purposes but agreed to use a dozen of them to carry passengers during peacetime, even this $3.6 million outlay would be a sunk cost that should not be double-counted. A dozen conversion sets would allow AMC to reduce the international passenger buy by $50 million a year. This conversion could thus be cost-effective by allowing strategic airlifters to generate both flying hours and revenue at the same time as opposed to flying empty to generate flying hours only.

It would be even more advantageous to use KC-10s as dedicated passenger carriers because C-17s are better suited to carrying cargo, while KC-10s have a larger passenger-carrying capacity. KC-10s are currently flown 5000 hours per year for cargo delivery. In times of shortage, AMC should switch C-17s to this cargo-flying role and equip some KC-10s to spend those 5000 hours carrying passengers instead.

In a separate study, we found that CRAF, being untrained and unequipped for protection, will be unable or unwilling to fly to airfields that are threatened by chemical, biological, or even high-precision conventional weapons. Some potential U.S. adversaries, such as Iraq and North Korea, have now developed these weapons and are likely to have more and better ones in the future. We proposed that CRAF fly to the nearest safe airfields and transload its cargo and passengers to organic assets, which would then fly the last leg into the conflict area. This plan calls for organic, dedicated passenger-carrying aircraft both tactical and strategic, for wartime use. Moreover, immediately after the September 11 attacks, civil aircraft were grounded. If AMC had aircraft that could carry a large number of passengers, they could be useful for urgent travel, including that of rescue personnel.

Make Nonpaying Passengers Pay

Military service personnel and their dependents currently fly free on military and AMC-chartered commercial flights when empty seats are available. This fringe benefit should be borne by the individual services, not by AMC alone. Nonpaying passengers should be charged a fare of, say, $100 on average per one-way trip. If the services reimbursed their personnel and dependents, the load factor would be unchanged and AMC would still receive $24 million a year for carrying these previously nonpaying passengers. Even if nonpaying passengers had to pay the fare themselves, the load factor and revenue might not be greatly affected, as most of these flights are overseas trips for which a $100 fare is still a bargain. If AMC were allowed to sell these seats to non-DoD government personnel as well, its revenue could be further increased.

Decide Whether to Allow AMC Limited Participation in Commercial Air Delivery

The need to conduct cost-effective air mobility operations for national security purposes could justify limited AMC participation in the commercial air delivery of cargo and passengers. AMC often flies organic assets partially or totally empty, particularly during return flights. It would help AMC financially to be able to deliver commercial cargo and passengers for a fee whenever its organic or chartered commercial flights were not full. Because of AMC's restricted route structure and service-quality considerations, the commercial airlift industry is unlikely to lose much business to AMC. To ensure that that is the case, the U.S. government could set an upper limit—say, $100 million to $200 million per year—on AMC commercial business.

AMC should examine its route structure and competitiveness to determine where and how often it can offer commercial services on its existing flights. On the other hand, letting the military participate in commerce, even if highly restricted, is a drastic step both politically and philosophically. We do not recommend such a program at this time. Rather, the government should estimate the program's benefit and decide whether AMC should be allowed to participate in the commercial air delivery business in such a restricted manner.

Competitively Price Organic Services

Staying competitive would confer two advantages. First, AMC customers would have fewer incentives to bypass AMC and seek airlift services elsewhere. A stable customer base would help AMC generate enough flying hours for its own pilots. Second, even under competitive pricing, AMC would continue to show an annual loss for its operations because it has large but legitimate "war readiness" costs that commercial air carriers do not. Yet the change in this annual operating loss over time becomes an effective measure of cost containment and quality improvement. AMC needs such an objective measure for improving the cost-effectiveness of its operations.

AMC should price certain airlift services low to be competitive even when its reimbursements do not fully cover its marginal or variable expenses in providing those services. Offering services that afford valuable training experience, albeit with only partial reimbursement, is less costly to AMC than arranging dedicated training missions without any reimbursement at all. AMC should continue to improve its quality of service. In the meantime, when certain services are still inferior in terms of on-time delivery or passenger comfort, prices should be lowered to stay competitive.

Competitive pricing would also allow AMC to charge customers a higher price to recoup the full cost (both fixed and variable) of unique and valuable services such as airlifting outsize cargo that commercial carriers cannot accommodate. This is an avenue for increasing airlift revenue to support AMC operations.

AMC should also charge one single, competitive price for the same service. It should eliminate the price differentials among the current three categories of customers: DoD, non-DoD U.S., and non-U.S customers.

SUGGESTED CORRECTIVE MEASURES TO DEAL WITH PROBLEMS OTHER THAN THE FLYING-HOUR SHORTAGE AND REVENUE LOSS

The measures described above will not only help address AMC's flying-hour shortage and revenue loss but also mitigate the other problems it faces.

Congress Should Allow AMC to Vary the Number of Authorized Pilots

The actual number of CPs during FY 2001 exceeded the authorized number by only 49 out of a total of 948, while the number of ACs exceeded those authorized by 29 out of a total of 949. The salary savings that would accrue from eliminating these positions would be about $5.1 million per year. This is not a large sum, especially considering the toll it would take on morale if these pilots were reassigned or laid off. Congress should thus allow AMC some flexibility in deviating from the number of pilots authorized provided that AMC makes compensatory adjustments in other budgetary items to keep its overall operational expenses within the bounds of congressional authorizations.

Congress Should Formally Allow AMC to Vary the Mix of Authorized Copilots and Aircraft Commanders

Bringing actual CP/AC ratios into accord with those authorized for airlifters would amount to replacing 66 CPs with ACs. This would result in an annual salary-cost increase of $1 million. On the other hand, a CP is required to fly many more hours per month than is an AC. Because a flying-hour shortage will recur from time to time, replacing 66 CPs with ACs would significantly reduce the flying-hour need. The flying-cost savings for just one hour per month for 66 CPs would be $2.7 million, which exceeds the $1 million annual salary cost. Thus, lowering the CP/AC ratios for airlifters to those authorized will give AMC added flexibility in managing the required number of flying hours.

For tankers, whose actual CP/AC ratios for FY 2001 were below those authorized, the salary savings in matching actual with authorized ratios would be $800,000 a year. However, just one extra flying hour per month for all of the 55 additional CPs would cost $2.1 million, which exceeds the $800,000 salary savings. Therefore, AMC might not want to meet authorized ratios for tankers.

Instead of generally not enforcing the authorized mix of CPs and ACs, Congress should formally allow AMC to vary the mix as long as the variation does not increase total authorized operational expenses, including salaries and training. AMC is in a better position than Congress to optimize this mix.

Flying-Hour Shortage Corrective Measures Would Increase Piloting During Training

Once the measures suggested above return AMC to plentiful flying hours even during lean-demand years, the number of pilots per flight can be reduced so that each will have more opportunity to pilot as opposed to merely observing others piloting.

AMC Should Reduce and Adapt to Deviations from Flying Plan

To reduce deviations from the flying plan, AMC should improve its projection capability and more frequently update this plan. It can also decrease commercial fixed buys and increase commercial expansion buys in its plan for the fiscal year. When AMC is running short on flying hours during a given fiscal year, it can reduce expansion buys and fly more itself for the remainder of the year. Equally important, AMC should accept deviation as a viable means of training for quick responses.

AMC Should Contract Out and Adapt to More Engagement Missions

AMC can contract out more of its engagement missions. At the same time, however, it should treat these missions as training for quick responses.

Recommended Measures Would Increase Reimbursement for Training

Competitive pricing and improved service quality will help AMC retain customers and halt the decline in the reimbursable share of its operating and training expenses. Competitive pricing adjusted for service quality establishes clear incentives for AMC to reduce costs and retain business. Moreover, once AMC makes equitable arrangements with commercial air carriers for reduced commercial buys when flying-hour shortages occur and uses its dedicated passenger-carrying capability for new business, it can retain more reimbursable cargo and passenger business in house.

TOWARD COST-EFFECTIVE AIR MOBILITY OPERATIONS

The peacetime demand for air mobility operations continues to exhibit wide fluctuation, sometimes too high and at other times too low for organic flying. Moreover, the wartime requirement for air mobility is on the rise, generating more asymmetry in wartime and peacetime demand. This asymmetry makes a flying-hour shortage even more likely, as an increase in the number of pilots needed for wartime will necessitate more flying hours for training during peacetime. Although AMC has been taking action to meet fluctuating airlift demand during peacetime, we have proposed additional corrective measures for generating new business and flying for AMC when shortages recur and for gaining flexibility in using commercial air carriers to smooth the demand for organic assets. These measures also include some that would make AMC services more competitive with commercial services. Such corrective measures should help AMC meet peacetime demand and maintain wartime readiness in a cost-effective manner.

ACKNOWLEDGMENTS

The author would like to thank a number of people for providing data and historical background. Craig Vara at AMC/DOT assembled the annual flying hours by CPs and by ACs and answered the author's many inquiries about the patterns of air mobility operations. Phil Widincamp and Thomas Grenham at AMC/DOTR provided the author with annual spreadsheets of the flying-hour program and selected AMC flying-hour execution reports. Judith Greene at AMC/DOY provided data on commercial fixed and expansion buys. Tommy Young at AMC/HO filled the author's requests for selected pages of historic data from old *Command Data Books* that are not readily available.

Tim Bonds and Michael Kennedy at RAND offered valuable comments and suggestions throughout the study. Finally, the report benefited greatly from the comments and suggestions of its reviewers, John Koehler and, especially, Marc Robbins.

ACRONYMS

AC	Aircraft commander
AMC	Air Mobility Command
AMPAS	Air Mobility Performance Analysis System
APOD	Aerial port of debarkation
APOE	Aerial port of embarkation
AWACS	Airborne Warning and Control System
BAI	Backup aircraft inventory
CD2	Channel Door to Door [program]
CINC	Commander in chief
COMALOC	Commercial Air Line of Communications
CP	Copilot
CRAF	Civil Reserve Air Fleet
DoD	Department of Defense
DVD	Direct Vendor Delivery
FY	Fiscal year
GSA	General Services Administration
GTP	Greater than planned
JA/ATT	Joint airdrop/air transportability training
JCSE	Joint Chiefs of Staff exercises

l.s.	Level of significance
MILALOC	Military Air Line of Communications
MRS	Mobility Requirements Study
MRS-BURU	Mobility Requirements Study Bottom-Up Review Update
MTM/D	Millions of ton-miles per day
MTW	Major theater war
O&M	Operation and maintenance
QDR	Quadrennial Defense Review
OEF	Operation Enduring Freedom
OPTEMPO	Operations tempo
PAA	Primary aircraft authorized
PAX	Passengers
PSFRs	Pilot Semiannual Flying Requirements
REMIS	Reliability Maintenance Information System
SAAM	Special assignment airlift mission
SDMI	Strategic Distribution Management Initiative
t	Standardized *t*-test statistic
TAA	Total aircraft authorized
TTF	Test, training, and ferry
TWCF	Transportation Working Capital Fund
UPT	Undergraduate Pilot Training
USTRANSCOM	U.S. Transportation Command
WWX	Worldwide Express

Chapter One

INTRODUCTION

The September 11 attacks and the 2001 Quadrennial Defense Review (QDR) have led the Department of Defense (DoD) leadership to change its terms of reference for sizing its force. Specifically, this approach has shifted from fighting two overlapping major theater wars (MTWs) in Northeast and Southwest Asia to one of (1) defending the United States; (2) swiftly defeating aggression in overlapping major conflict while preserving the option to call for a decisive victory in one of those conflicts; and (3) conducting a limited number of smaller-scale contingency operations.[1] Although the new force planning is still being studied, it has become clear that the objectives of U.S. peacetime air mobility operations—to meet peacetime demand and maintain wartime readiness—will remain unchanged.[2]

The ideal intensity of peacetime operations lies between a level that is not too high to stress personnel and aircraft and one that is not so low as to provide insufficient flying for pilot training. However, there is an inherent ambiguity in the terms *peacetime* and *wartime*. For the purpose of this study, we define peacetime as periods in which the overall air mobility demand is low. This occurs when there is no major conflict and/or there are no smaller-scale contingencies that together demand high-mobility support. Conversely, we define wartime as periods in which the mobility demand is higher than that in peacetime. During wartime, the United States would be involved in a major conflict and/or one or more smaller-scale contingencies that together would call for high-mobility support. We set the peacetime/wartime demarcation at the intensity level of Operation Enduring Freedom (OEF), at or above which the period is considered wartime.[3]

[1]See *Quadrennial Defense Review Report*, Washington, D.C.: U.S. Department of Defense, September 30, 2001, p. 17.

[2]"Wartime readiness" means that the United States has sufficient personnel and assets to serve and meet wartime requirements.

[3]In contrast, although the Kosovo air war is considered by some—especially many at the Air Combat Command—to be another MTW, we consider it peacetime as far as air mobility activities

Today's adversaries, although much less potent than the former Soviet Union, are more prone to take hostile action against U.S. interests. Such actions led to Operation Desert Shield/Desert Storm during 1990–1991 and to subsequent U.S. involvement in Iraq and elsewhere.[4] The heightened intensity and frequency of U.S. peacetime missions in the 1990s have been well recognized. During FY 2000 and FY 2001, however, the Air Mobility Command (AMC) faced a problem that had not appeared in recent years: Its air mobility activities were reduced to such an extent that its flying hours were no longer sufficient to satisfy copilots' aging requirement.[5,6] Like any sizable contingency in the past, OEF has eliminated this flying-hour shortage. When OEF ends, however, such a shortage is likely to recur from time to time. AMC thus needs to develop the flexibility to meet fluctuating demand, both high and low, without sacrificing training and readiness. Indeed, gaining flexibility is consistent with the 2001 QDR's new "basis of defense planning from a 'threat-based' model that has dominated thinking in the past to a 'capabilities-based' model for the future."[7] Because the United States cannot predict when and how often war might occur, it is important to have the flexibility to meet fluctuating demand.

---

are concerned. It was of short duration (taking place between March 24 and June 10, 1999) and involved few Army operations. Moreover, its airlift demand was below that of OEF.

[4]Generally, whether a year is fiscal or calendar will be made evident in this report. Where neither is specified, fiscal year is intended.

[5]When the international situation is relative calm, U.S. involvement is reduced (a situation that the U.S. government strives to achieve). In addition, there is increased competition from commercial carriers for AMC business.

[6]AMC expects a CP of a particular aircraft type to fly, on average, a specific number of hours per month. This "aging rate" allows CPs to be promoted to a higher rank within a reasonable time. While aircraft commanders (ACs) are also expected to fly a certain number of hours to maintain flying proficiency, those hours are in the teens per month and are far below the aging rate for CPs. ACs have little problem attaining this proficiency rate. In this report, we call these rates *the aging requirement* for CPs and the *proficiency requirement* for ACs. Both are expectations and planning factors that are designed to allow pilots to be promoted on time and maintain flying currency.

This study focuses on pilots who fly full time—i.e., those for whom flying as opposed to working behind a desk is their principal duty. Full-time pilots are classified into two categories. An AC is a pilot who can serve as the ranking officer of the aircrew. A CP is not qualified to command a flight and must be accompanied by an AC on a flight. The category of AC includes three crew positions: aircraft commander, instructor pilot, and flight examiner. The category of CP includes copilot and first pilot. That a category and a crew position have the same name can be confusing. Because these names are already in common use in the military, however, we decided not to introduce new names for the two categories. To reduce confusion, we use the terms *CP* and *AC* to refer to their respective categories in this report. In the rare occasions when these terms are used to represent crew positions, we will explicitly indicate as such.

[7]See *Quadrennial Defense Review Report*, September 30, 2001, p. iv.

ISSUES EXAMINED

This study compares the peacetime tempo of air mobility operations in the Cold War (1980s) and post–Cold War (1990s) periods[8] and examines the factors and associated trends that can affect AMC's ability to meet these dual objectives cost-effectively. The study does not, however, examine whether AMC has enough manpower and hardware to meet its wartime and peacetime missions. Rather, it seeks to ascertain whether AMC has the flexibility to generate enough flying hours for pilot training when flying demand is low. Can AMC man flying operations with the number of pilots authorized by Congress? How well does the actual ratio of copilots (CPs) to aircraft commanders (ACs) match what is authorized? Comparing peacetime operations in the 1980s with those of the 1990s, did pilots get less hands-on training during flights in the latter period? Was AMC less able to project airlift demand accurately in the latter than in the former period? Did AMC have to fly more missions with shorter advance notice? Has AMC been successful in using reimbursements from its customers to defray its operating expenses?

This study uses a number of measures to identify potential problems. In Chapter Two, we analyze whether the flying hours of key organic (AMC-owned)[9] assets (the C-5, C-141, C-17, C-130, KC-135, and KC-10) have been increasing since 1981. The C-5, C-141, and C-17 are AMC's strategic airlifters, while the C-130 is its tactical airlifter. The KC-135 and KC-10 constitute AMC's tanker force.[10] Organic aircraft fly much less often than do commercial aircraft. Some increased flying would not overstress the aircraft but would imply higher expenses in returning aircraft to their wartime readiness status. We also examine the flying hours per pilot of a given aircraft type and study whether there is any shortage in flying hours for pilot training.

In Chapter Three, we examine the mix of CPs and ACs who are flying full time at AMC. We first determine whether AMC is able to man flying operations with

---

[8]The peacetime period in the 1990s does not include the Gulf-War–affected years, FY 1990 and FY 1991, or 1994, a unique year in which many C-141s were grounded because of possible weep-hole cracks in their wings. This grounding is described in Chapter Two.

[9]"Organic" means "AMC owned." Organic assets are AMC-owned assets, and organic flying hours are flying hours flown on AMC-owned assets.

[10]The KC-135, a military version of the Boeing 707, is used to refuel aircraft while in flight. A small number of KC-135s have been modified to carry some 10 tons of cargo apiece. The KC-10 is a military version of the DC-10. Although it was designed as a tanker, DoD plans to use some of them to carry about 40 tons of standard-size pallets of cargo in the event of a conflict. See Congressional Budget Office, *Moving U.S. Forces: Options for Strategic Mobility*, Washington, D.C., February 1997, pp. 12–13. Unlike military cargo aircraft such as the C-5, C-141, C-17, and C-130, KC-135 and KC-10 tankers are modified versions of civil aircraft: They have low wings, and their cargo doors are higher off the ground. In addition, special elevators are required for loading and unloading. These aircraft are, however, cheaper per copy because both they and their civil counterparts are produced in large quantities.

the number of pilots authorized by Congress. If the actual number of CPs and ACs exceeds those authorized by Congress, should that number be reduced?

We then compare the actual CP/AC ratio with that authorized. If the actual ratio is greater than the authorized ratio, there may be too many CPs relative to ACs. Alternatively, there may not be enough ACs to command all aircraft, since every flight requires at least one AC. On the other hand, if the actual ratio is less than that authorized, there may be too few CPs relative to ACs—or there may be flights with more than one AC, which would involve more salary cost because ACs earn a higher average salary than do CPs. At the same time, an AC can fly significantly less than a CP and still meet his proficiency requirement. We will show that this flying-cost savings can easily outstrip the higher salary cost involved such that having relatively more ACs than CPs can be less expensive to maintain in an environment in which flying-hour shortages occur frequently.

In Chapter Four, we analyze whether pilots are spending less time piloting. During a flight, all working pilots in an aircraft can credit the hours of the flight toward their aging and proficiency requirements. However, it would be valuable to distinguish piloting hours (in which an individual is in a pilot seat piloting the aircraft) from observing hours (in which an individual is simply observing others piloting and is not in a pilot seat). Training experience is superior when it consists of more piloting hours and fewer observing hours.

AMC schedules all pilots and aircraft types to fly a given number of hours each year. In Chapter Five, we study the deviation of the actual flying of aircraft and pilots from that scheduled. The greater the deviation, the more difficult and costly it will be to change the flight schedule and the greater the effect will be of short-notice changes on pilots' quality of life.

Chapter Six examines whether commercial air carriers are capturing an increasing share of AMC customers' airlift business. In periods of flying-hour shortages, AMC may want to retain more airlift missions in house and contract fewer flying hours to commercial carriers.

Chapter Seven summarizes the potential problems identified in Chapters Two through Six. Finally, in Chapter Eight, we suggest solutions.

DATA SOURCES

Two sources can be used to provide data for analyzing the issues above. The Air Mobility Performance Analysis System (AMPAS) obtains data from command posts worldwide. Pilots report flight data to a command post when they land at an airfield. There are three reasons we do not use this source for our analyses. First, 1980s data are no longer available, and we wish to compare the operations tempo (OPTEMPO) in the 1990s (the post–Cold War era) to the 1980s (the Cold War era). Second, the all-important Flying-Hour Program statistics are not derived from these data, although official documents such as AMC's annual *Command Data Book* rely heavily on numbers in the program. Thus, using AMPAS would mean using data that are not necessarily consistent with these authoritative documents. Third, the AMPAS data seem to have errors and inconsistencies, such as flying hours that are obviously far too numerous even for a fully fueled aircraft and negative flying hours documented for certain flights. Moreover, if a tanker (a KC-135 or KC-10) is to be in the theater for a long time, the control of the aircraft may be transferred to the field commander, and the flying hours in the theater will not be recorded in AMPAS. This could result in a significant underestimation of the flying hours for these aircraft.

An alternative data source is the Reliability Maintenance Information System (REMIS), which collects flight data from pilots' Form 781. Official flying hours, including those that appear in the *Command Data Book*, are based on REMIS data. A comparison of OPTEMPO in the Cold War and post–Cold War periods was feasible because we could access data from 1981 forward. We did not find any significant errors in the flying-hour data derived from REMIS, and, as expected, the flying-hour data are very similar to those in the authoritative annual *Command Data Book*. For these reasons, we chose REMIS over AMPAS as the data source for this study. In subsequent chapters, we will describe additional data used in specific analyses. When different sources of data were available, we selected the data that appeared in official AMC documents or that were directly provided by AMC offices.

For the figures and tables in this study, we used data at least as late as FY 1999 and, for many, FY 2000. For the most important ones, we obtained data that included all of FY 2001 and the first four months of FY 2002.

Chapter Two

IS AMC FLYING LESS?

In the 1990s, the number of Air Force active-duty military personnel declined by 40 percent.[1] During this period, the Air Force was deployed on a continual basis in Northeast and Southwest Asia. It was also deployed for peacekeeping in Bosnia and for evacuation operations and humanitarian assistance in Somalia, Bangladesh, Thailand, Cambodia, Rwanda, and Ethiopia.[2] Many believe that this increased commitment, coupled with reduced resources, placed added stress on Air Force aircraft and personnel.

This belief may not apply to AMC for three reasons. First, the decline in AMC's assets might not have been as large as the 40 percent drop in the number of personnel for the Air Force overall. The number of strategic airlifters in AMC (the C-5, C-141, and C-17) did decrease by 44 percent between 1981 and 1999 (see Figure 2.1).[3] In many circumstances, however, airlift capacity is a better measure of overall capacity than number of airlifters. Because the newer C-17 has a larger capacity than the retiring C-141, for example, the strategic airlift capacity of AMC can be said to have dropped by only 24 percent to 35 percent, depending on whether Air Force capacity-planning factors or Gulf War experience[4] is used to convert number of aircraft to airlift capacity.[5] The number of

---

[1]This figure is based on a comparison of the number of personnel in 1999 with those in 1984.

[2]See Richard Beery, *Is the Expeditionary Aerospace Force the Right Approach for the Air Force as We Enter the 21st Century?* Fort Leavenworth, KS: School of Advanced Military Studies, United States Army Command and General Staff College, May 27, 1999, p. 6.

[3]These data appeared in annual issues of the *Command Data Book*, Scott Air Force Base, IL: Headquarters Air Mobility Command, Manpower and Innovation Flight.

[4]The planning factors used by the Air Force based on Gulf War experience appeared in Jean Gebman, Lois Batchelder, and Katherine Poehlmann, *Finding the Right Mix of Military and Civil Airlift: Issues and Implications, Volume 2, Analysis*, MR-406/2-AF, Santa Monica: RAND, 1994, pp. 11 and 134. The airlift capacity for each type of aircraft in millions of ton-miles per day (MTM/D) is calculated by multiplying the following planning factors: speed (knots), utilization rate (hours per day), payload (tons per aircraft), productivity (miles with cargo versus miles without cargo), and number of aircraft.

[5]See Figures A.1 and A.2 in the appendix. The Air Force has also entered into a follow-on agreement with Boeing for an additional 60 C-17s, bringing the fleet's total from 120 to 180. This addition is

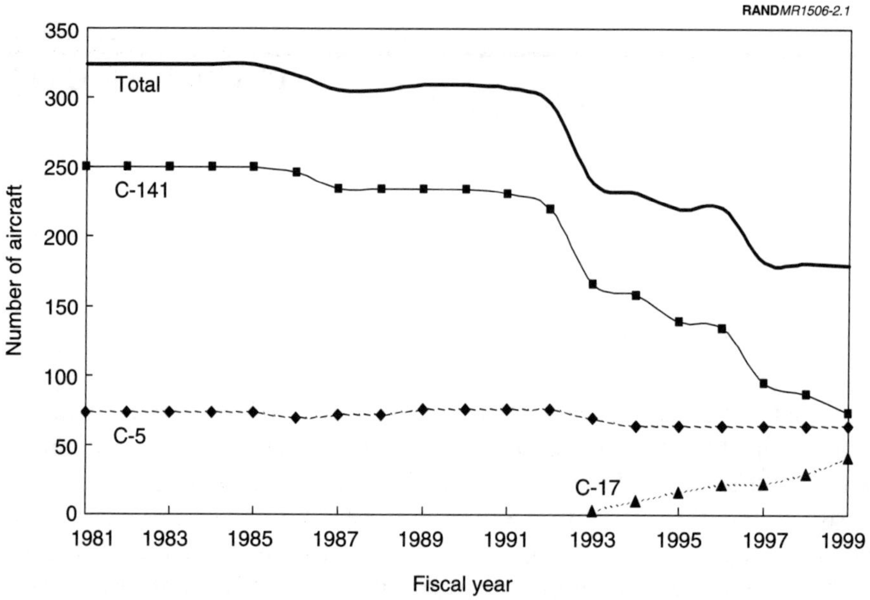

Figure 2.1—The Number of Strategic Airlifters Has Decreased Sharply Since 1992

strategic airlift pilots declined by 25 percent between 1982 and 2000 (see Figure 2.2).

Second, peacetime operations for fighters and bombers differ from those for airlifters and tankers. Both are heavily involved in routine deliveries of personnel, supplies, and equipment to overseas bases even in the absence of small-scale contingencies. In the 1990s, however, the number of major U.S. military installations abroad declined by almost 75 percent[6] and active-duty military personnel abroad decreased by 50 percent,[7] significantly reducing the demand on airlifters and tankers for routine deliveries. Moreover, when contingency activities are high, AMC has the flexibility to hire commercial air carriers to share air mobility chores. In the opposite situation, when contingency activities are low, AMC can reduce commercial augmentation to retain flying hours for the training and aging of its pilots. In contrast, aside from some training

expected to more than compensate for the C-141's retirement and to continue the uptrend in total airlift capability that began in 1997. In fact, Major General Arthur Lichte, AMC's Chief of Plans and Programs, said, "It's our command's position that we would want 222 C-17s or more." (See "Despite Heavy Demands, AMC Predicts No Change in Airlift Requirement," *Inside the Air Force*, March 8, 2002.) The 42 or more C-17s, on top of the 60 aircraft recently bought, will further enhance the uptrend.

[6]See Figure A.3 in the appendix.

[7]See Figure A.4 in the appendix.

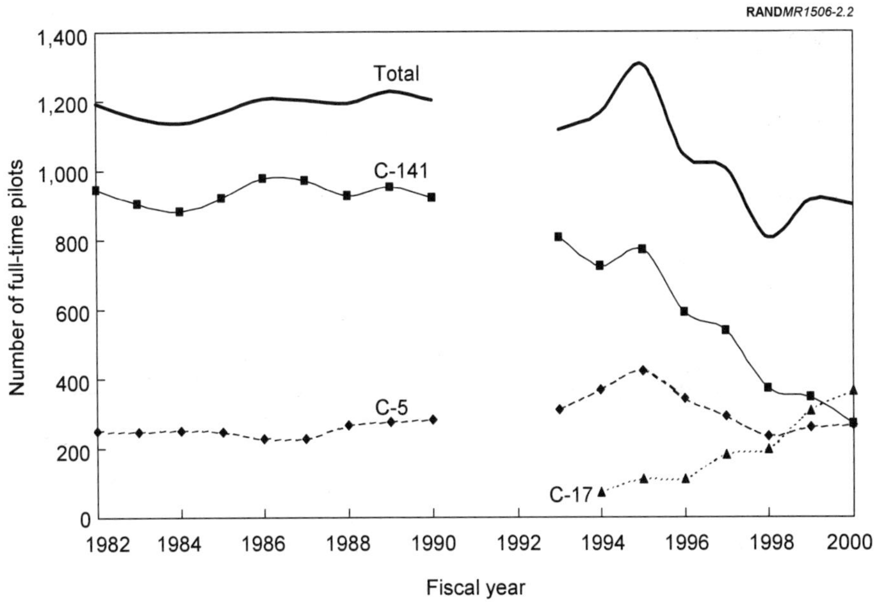

Figure 2.2—The Number of Strategic Airlift Pilots Declined in the Mid-1990s

missions, the overall annual intensity of fighters and bombers depends on the frequency and level of contingency deployments. In the absence of special deployments, in other words, fighter and bomber units have fewer routine activities and do not have a commercial counterpart to help share their burden. Thus, the overall intensity of AMC peacetime operations can be less sensitive to special deployments and hence more stable through the years.

Third, although the total peacetime airlift operations in the 1990s seemed numerous and intensive, they should be compared to those during the 1980s to determine whether resources were truly more stressed.

This chapter addresses the question, Is AMC flying more or less? Although this question would appear to be straightforward, simple answers with plots of annual flying hours over time ignore how many aircraft and pilots are involved. Figure 2.3 shows three such curves for strategic airlifters (the C-5, C-141, and C-17), tactical airlifters (the C-130), and tankers (the KC-135 and KC-10), respectively. Thus, it would be better to pose the questions, Is AMC flying more per aircraft, and is AMC flying more per pilot? Even these questions, however, are too broad, as a C-141 would differ from its replacement, the C-17, both in capacity and in other characteristics. Also, an airlifter's function is very different from that of a tanker. Yet an examination of flying hours per aircraft

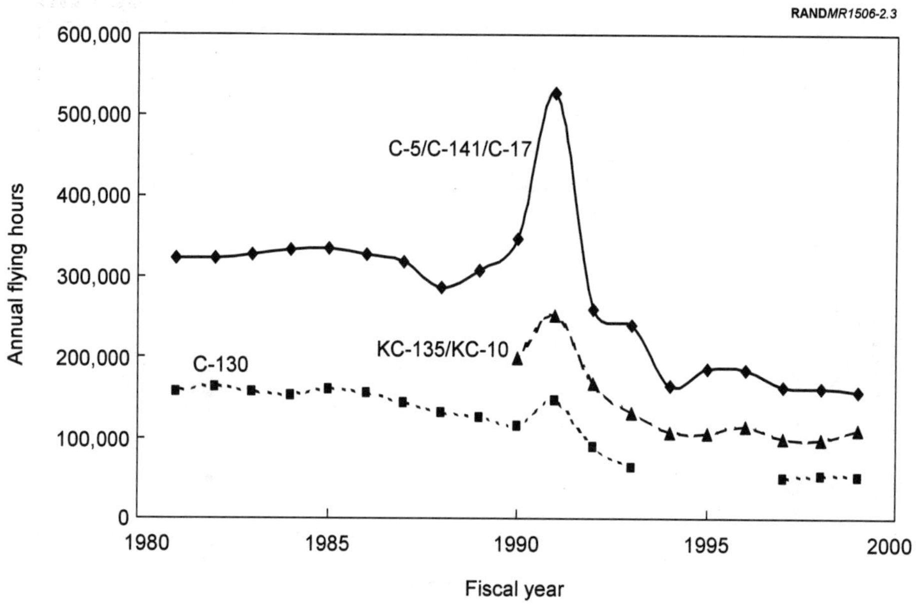

NOTE: The reasons for the missing 1980s data for the tankers and the mid-1990s data for C-130s will be given later in the chapter.

Figure 2.3—Annual Flying Hours for Airlifters and Tankers

for all aircraft types would not reveal the hours of a retiring aircraft decreasing or those of a newly deployed aircraft increasing. One must therefore refine the question as follows: Is AMC flying more per aircraft within a given aircraft type? Similarly, is AMC flying more per pilot within a given aircraft type?

We will use three measures to assess AMC flying: (1) the annual flying hours per aircraft of a given type during peacetime; (2) the monthly flying hours per CP of a given aircraft type during peacetime; and (3) the monthly flying hours per AC of a given aircraft type during peacetime. We have separated the data for CPs and ACs to reflect differences in flying requirements.

ANNUAL FLYING HOURS PER AIRCRAFT

The flying-hour data given herein are based on the annual spreadsheets of the Flying-Hour Program provided by Phil Widincamp, AMC/DOT. Figures 2.4 and 2.5 show the annual flying hours for AMC-owned C-5s and C-141s, respectively, from FY 1981 to FY 1999. Both figures show the highest number of flying hours in 1991, a period that includes the Gulf War. Although we show all data points

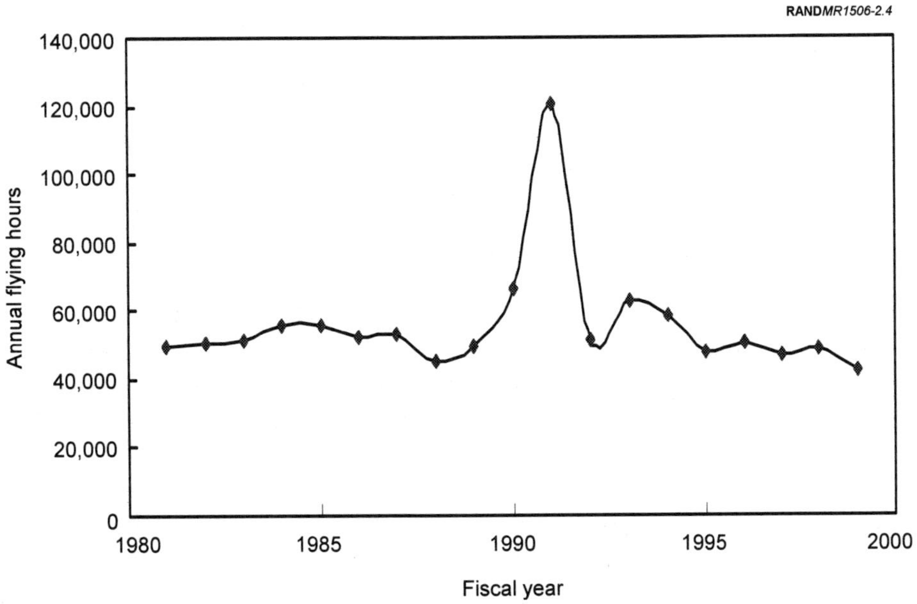

Figure 2.4—C-5 Annual Flying Hours

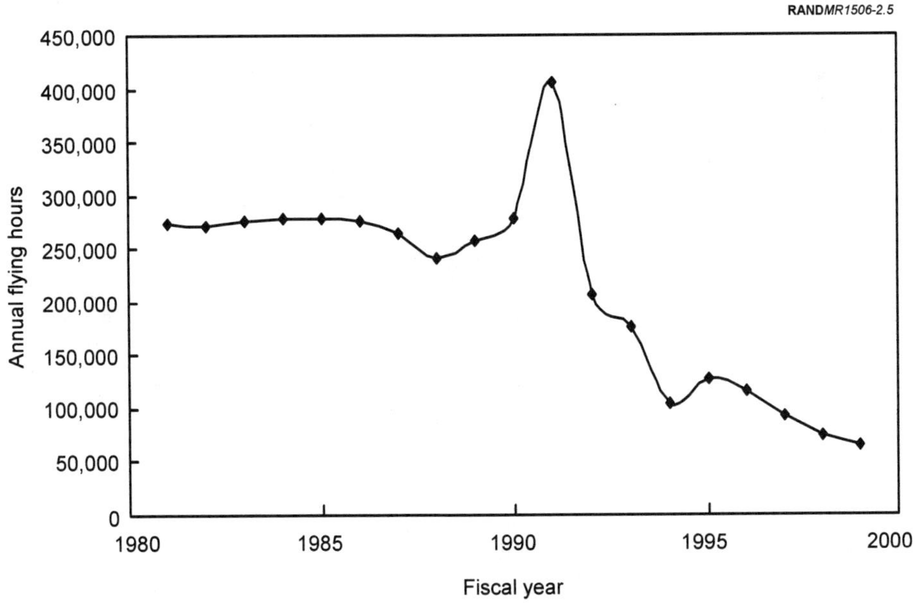

Figure 2.5—C-141 Annual Flying Hours

on these and subsequent graphs, we exclude the 1990 and 1991 data points[8] in our determination of peacetime trend lines in subsequent graphs because our purpose is to examine peacetime, not wartime, OPTEMPO.

In 1994, a dip occurred in the total number of annual flying hours of C-5s, C-141s, and C-17s (see Figure 2.3). This raises the question of whether the 1994 data point should be included in the determination of peacetime trend lines. On May 14, 1993, after the Air Force Scientific Advisory Board reported that the weep-hole cracks in C-141 wings were more extensive than had previously been estimated, General Ronald Fogelman restricted all 260 C-141s in the active and reserve forces to a maximum payload of 55,000 pounds, or about 14,000 pounds below normal peacetime loads.[9] On August 9, 1993, General Fogelman also grounded 45 C-141Bs and restricted another 116 from in-flight refueling. By November 30, 1994, the weep-hole repair had been completed on all C-141s. Because the C-141 wing crack was as rare an event as an MTW and resulted in a large drop in C-141 flying during 1994 (see Figure 2.5), we excluded the incident from our peacetime trend analysis. Thus, while the 1994 data point will continue to be shown in subsequent graphs, it is not included in the determination of trend lines.[10] It should be noted that if the 1994 data point were included, the resulting trend lines would not change significantly. In sum, while all annual data points will be displayed in the graphs throughout this report, FYs 1990, 1991, and 1994 will be excluded in the determination of peacetime trend lines.[11]

By contrast, we did include the Kosovo air war (which took place between March 24 and June 10, 1999) as part of peacetime operations because it did not involve any large-scale ground operations. Without a large airlift requirement for Army operations, the airlift intensity of the Kosovo conflict was far below

---

[8]On August 2, 1990, Iraq invaded Kuwait, and on August 7 President Bush issued a deployment order sending U.S. forces, including airlifters and tankers, to the Persian Gulf. On January 17, 1991, allied forces began Operation Desert Storm, and Kuwait was liberated on February 26. The data points in Figure 2.4 were based on total flying hours on a fiscal-year basis. Because FY 1990 covers the period from October 1, 1989, to September 30, 1990, its data point includes flying hours during the initial two months of the buildup (August and September 1990).

[9]See *The Air Mobility Command 1993 Historical Highlights*, Scott Air Force Base, IL: Air Mobility Command, Office of History, 1994.

[10]C-141 operational impacts were much smaller in FY 1993 and FY 1995 than in FY 1994. We can interpret the impacts on FY 1993 and FY 1995 as part of "normal" peacetime operations, so the data points for these two years need not be excluded in the determination of trend lines.

[11]For each of the figures and tables in this report showing trend lines, averages, or rates of change, there will be a note indicating which years' data points were excluded from the determination. We adopt the convention that if the data points for FYs 1990, 1991, and/or 1994 were not available in the first place, we do not mention that they are excluded, because there is nothing to exclude. In Figure 4.1, for example, data made available to us include those for FY 1990 and FY 1994 (represented by open symbols in the figure) but not for FY 1991. Thus, the corresponding note will read that data points for 1990 and 1994 were excluded from the determination of the trend lines.

what an MTW such as the Gulf War would have demanded and also fell below that of OEF, our demarcation for peacetime and wartime.[12] As far as airlift is concerned, we therefore treated the Kosovo air war as a small-scale contingency that did not demand high air mobility support and included it in our trend analysis of peacetime operations.

Data on the number of AMC-owned aircraft (primary aircraft authorized, or PAA) in the inventory by type and by year from 1980 to 1999 were obtained from the annual *Command Data Books*.[13] Figure A.5 shows the PAA aircraft inventory for the C-5 as well as for other aircraft. On the basis of the data shown in Figure 2.4, we calculated actual flying hours per aircraft.[14] During the 1990s (excluding 1990, 1991, and 1994), the average number of flying hours per year per C-5 was 756 hours.[15] The regression line shows an increase of 3.3 hours per year. If we use the average number of annual flying hours of 700 during 1981–1989 as our base, however, we find that this increase was 0.5 percent per year (see Figure 2.6).[16] One might not consider this increase negligible because annual flying hours could increase 10 percent over the two decades. More signifi-

[12]The air mobility intensity of OEF is higher than that of the Kosovo air war in terms of both total flying hours for the campaign and monthly flying hours per aircraft during the campaign.

[13]In this study, we measure the number of aircraft in units of PAA. The numbers of PAA belonging to AMC has appeared in the authoritative annual *Command Data Books* over the past two decades. PAA is the number of operating aircraft that are authorized to be staffed with aircrews. On the other hand, some might prefer to use total aircraft authorized (TAA). TAA is the sum of PAA and backup aircraft inventory (BAI), while BAI is the number of spare or backup aircraft that can be operational but are not budgeted for aircrews. Unfortunately, for large portions of the past two decades, TAA numbers are available only in aggregate over different commands; in other words, they are not segregated for AMC. Yet this study seeks to compare the peacetime operation of AMC assets during the Cold War and post–Cold War periods. We employed those TAA numbers that are available on AMC to repeat the calculation of flying hours per aircraft, and we then made a comparison to our results employing PAA. We noted little difference in the trends of flying hours per aircraft based on TAA or PAA. This comparison bolsters our findings based on PAA.

[14]See also Figure A.5 in the appendix. When we calculated annual flying hours per AMC aircraft, we included the flying hours of associate reservists, who do not have aircraft of their own and fly AMC aircraft. Moreover, all flying hours are included whether they are on operation and maintenance (O&M) missions or Transportation Working Capital Fund (TWCF) missions—e.g., channel, exercise, contingency, and special assignment airlift missions (SAAMs).

[15]There was a relatively large increase in flying hours for FY 1993. Indeed, actual monthly flying hours exceeded those planned from the start of that fiscal year. Operation Restore Hope, the United Nations–sanctioned military intervention in Somalia to safeguard the delivery of food to starving Somalis from December 9, 1992, to May 4, 1993, contributed to this increase. As discussed earlier, the restriction on C-141 maximum payload was announced on May 14, 1993, and the grounding and cessation of in-flight refueling of some C-141s on August 9, 1993. The first operational C-17s were introduced on June 4, 1993, and the C-17 fleet barely began to contribute to the flying duty during FY 1993. The combined effects of C-141s and C-17s also forced C-5s to fly more to compensate.

In addition to the FY 1990 and FY 1991 data points associated with the Gulf War, the FY 1994 data point was excluded in determining the peacetime trend line for the reasons discussed earlier.

[16]See also Table 2.1.

RANDMR1506-2.6

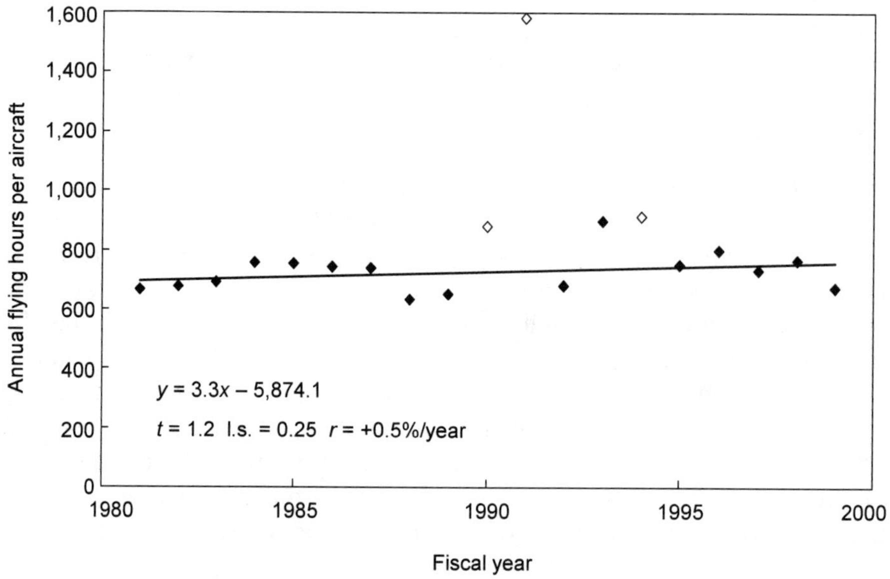

NOTE: Data points for 1990, 1991, and 1994 were excluded from the determination of the trend line.

Figure 2.6—C-5 Annual Flying Hours per Aircraft During Peacetime

cantly, however, Figure 2.6 shows that the trend is not statistically significant—that is, the increase of 0.5 percent per year is not significantly different from a 0 percent increase.[17] Therefore, there is no basis for arguing that the C-5 was flying more in the 1990s than in the 1980s.

---

[17]For all trend line analyses, we performed a *t*-test to determine whether the coefficient of the independent variable (the slope) is zero. The standardized *t*-test statistic (*t*), the level of significance (l.s.), and the rate (*r*) are shown below the regression equation. The l.s. is the probability of type I error, or the probability that the slope is actually zero . However, our sample results led us to erroneously reject a zero slope. Thus, the smaller the l.s., the smaller the probability that there is no trend or the higher our confidence that there is a nonzero trend. To highlight those likely nonzero trends in the figures and tables throughout the following chapters, we have boldfaced the *t*, l.s., and *r* numbers whenever the l.s. is 0.05 or less. In other words, there is a probability of 95 percent or higher that the trend or slope is not zero. To calculate the rate, we first determined the average annual value of the 1980s (or those years in the 1980s for which data were available) as the reference value or base. The rate is the annual change or the slope of the linear regression line divided by the average value (i.e., 3.3/700 = 0.5 percent in the current case). If there were no data for the 1980s, we used the average value for the years in the 1990s (excluding 1990, 1991, and 1994). It should also be noted that the regression software often gives the coefficients of the linear equations throughout this report more digits than their numbers of significant figures.

Table 2.1

Annual Flying Hours per Aircraft During Peacetime

Aircraft	Data Period (fiscal years)	Average During the 1990s (hours/ year–aircraft)	Rate of Change (%/year)	*t*-Test Statistic	Level of Significance
C-5	1981–1999	756	+0.5	1.2	0.25
C-141	1981–1999	929	**–1.3**	**6.2**	**0.00**
C-17	1994–1999	937	**+18.0**	**5.9**	**0.01**
C-130	1981–1999	609	–0.2	0.4	0.70
KC-135	1993–1999	388	–1.1	0.6	0.61
KC-10	1992–1999	748	–0.7	0.3	0.77

NOTE: Data points for 1990, 1991 and 1994 were excluded from the determination of the numbers in the third to sixth columns. Bold entries indicate that the probability of a nonzero trend (rate of change) is 95 percent or higher.

We similarly calculated annual flying hours per C-141, which are shown in Figure A.6 in the appendix and in Table 2.1.[18] The C-141 did not fly more in the 1990s, and its annual flying hours fell by 1.3 percent per year (see Table 2.1). The C-141 aircraft inventory was stable throughout the 1980s and until 1992. Thereafter, it declined quite rapidly, from 220 in 1992 to 74 in 1999 (See Figure A.5). However, even this seemingly sharp decline was less rapid than that in flying hours, thus causing a decline in flying hours per aircraft in the 1990s.

During 1995–1999, the annual flying hours per C-17 increased by 18 percent per year (see Table 2.1).[19] For a newly deployed aircraft, it is normal for annual flying hours per aircraft to increase initially. Moreover, the trend indicates that the flying hours per C-17 will be higher than those per C-141 or C-5.[20] However, more data points are needed to confirm this trend. The annual flying hours per C-130 did not increase over the past two decades (see Table 2.1).[21] Nor did those for the KC-135 and KC-10 (Table 2.1).[22]

Overall, none of the aircraft examined except the C-17 showed a statistically significant increase in annual flying hours per aircraft in the 1990s. Indeed, we found that C-5, C-141, and C-130—aircraft for which comparable data were

---

[18]For our analysis of each aspect of operations, we often show only the C-5 graph in the text and refer the reader to specific graphs in the appendix for other aircraft (the C-141, C-17, C-130, KC-135, and KC-10). However, we discuss the characteristics and trends of all these aircraft in the text. Moreover, for many statements made in the text, we refer to graphs in the appendix for data support.

[19]See also Figure A.7 in the appendix.

[20]See Figure A.7 in the appendix.

[21]See Figure A.8 in the appendix.

[22]See Figures A.9 and A.10 in the appendix.

available for the past two decades—were not flown more in the post–Cold War era than during the Cold War.

One might argue that the actual number of flying hours per aircraft is not relevant to AMC because military airlifters and tankers in any case fly far less than do their commercial equivalents, such as the B-747. These military aircraft can be flown substantially more per year without stressing the aircraft. However, more flying per year would increase the maintenance cost in returning aircraft to their wartime readiness status.

MONTHLY FLYING HOURS PER COPILOT

Thus far we have shown that aircraft did not fly more in the post–Cold War era than during the Cold War, but whether CPs and ACs have been subject to increased flying demand remains to be discussed.

Craig Vara at AMC/DOT provided us with annual data on the number of AMC CPs and ACs and their monthly flying hours. Figure 2.7 shows the monthly flying hours per C-5 CP.[23] The aging requirement for a C-5 CP is 30 flying hours per month. Over the past two decades, monthly flying hours showed no significant trend of either rising or declining and were on average slightly above the aging requirement. After the Cold War and the Gulf War, frequent peacetime contingencies and normal airlift activities yielded as much flying as C-5 CPs had experienced during the Cold War. However, lower overall peacetime demand from time to time and increased competition from commercial carriers can prevent CPs from meeting their aging requirement. In fact, the CPs of all six aircraft studied here had trouble meeting the requirement during FY 2000 and FY 2001. During FY 2000, average monthly flying hours per C-5 CP dropped to 26 (indicated as a star in Figure 2.7), well below the required 30 hours per month.

In general, the frequency and intensity of peacetime contingencies in the post–Cold War era are hard to predict and the counterterrorism initiative adopted after September 11 has not made such prediction any easier. Both variables will likely fluctuate so that for some years flying will be considerably below the aging requirement, while for other years it will be above. AMC's corrective measures for the recurring shortage of organic flying hours consist of cutting commercial augmentation, flying organic aircraft with lesser loads, and putting more CPs on

---

[23]Flying hours of any mission type or flying distance can be used to satisfy the aging or proficiency requirement. The trend line was based on data points from 1982 to 1999, excluding 1990, 1991, and 1994. For this and Figures A.11 to A.15, the determination of the trend lines was based on the annual data up to and including FY 1999.

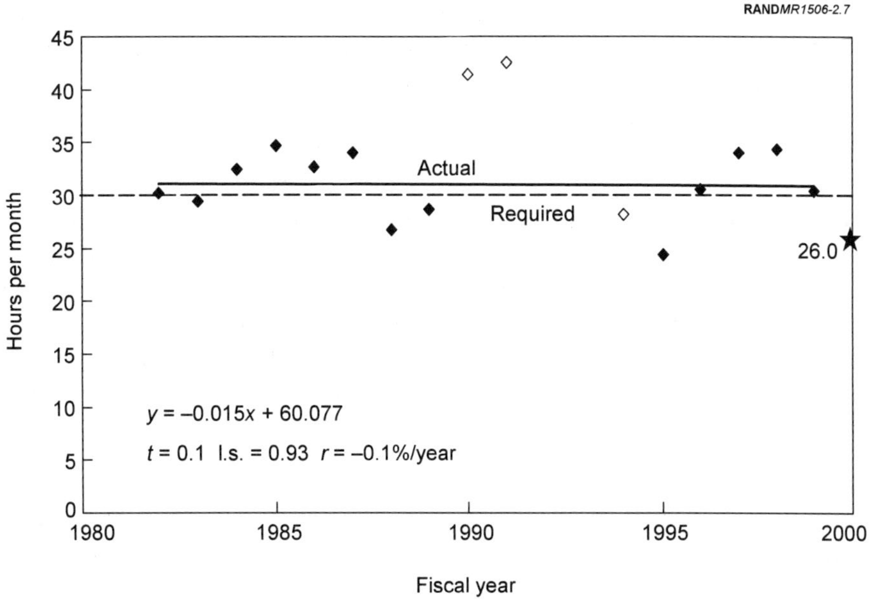

NOTE: Data points for 1990, 1991, 1994, and 2000 were excluded from the determination of the trend line.

Figure 2.7—C-5 Monthly Flying Hours per Copilot

a flight. Commercial augmentation is airlift business contracted to commercial carriers during peacetime. It has been used as an incentive to participate in the Civil Reserve Air Fleet (CRAF) to help meet wartime airlift requirements.[24]

---

[24]The CRAF program was established by a 1951 executive order. It was activated only during the Gulf War and cost $1.35 billion. It transported 62 percent of passengers and 27 percent of cargo during the deployment phase, as well as 84 percent of the returning passengers and 40 percent of cargo during the redeployment phase (bringing troops and equipment home after the completion of the ground campaign). CRAF Stage I could involve as many as 90 long-range international aircraft; Stage II, a cumulative total of 286 international, aeromedical, and national aircraft; and Stage III, 592 international, aeromedical, and national aircraft, including those in Stages I and II. (See Defense Science Board, *Report of the Defense Science Board Task Force on Strategic Mobility*, Washington, D.C., August 15, 1996, pp. 66–67.) The three stages of CRAF were intended to provide 19.5 MTM/D of the 49.7-MTM/D mobility requirement planned for major contingencies. Thus, CRAF could provide as much as 40 percent of the capability. The latest revision on requirements, the Mobility Requirements Study 2005 (MRS-05), calls for a minimum of 51.1 MTM/D, which is not significantly different from the 49.7 MTM/D determined during the Mobility Requirements Study Bottom-Up Review Update (MRS-BURU) in 1995. However, variations in assumptions examined in MRS-05 generated a range of airlift demands up to 67 MTM/D. (See MRS-05 Executive Summary and Transmittal Letter from Defense Secretary William Cohen to Congressman Bob Stump, Chairman of the House Committee on Armed Services, January 10, 2001.) As a prerequisite to CRAF membership, an air carrier must maintain minimum long-range international fleet commitment levels: at least a 3500-nautical-mile range and a 10-hour-per-day utilization rate, and at least 30 percent of its passenger fleet and 15 percent of its cargo fleet. (See *Fact Sheet on Civil Reserve Air Fleet*, Public Affairs Offices, Scott Air Force Base, IL: Air Mobility Command, August 1997.) With

When the demand for organic airlift unexpectedly drops during a fiscal year, AMC can reduce its commercial expansion buy and thus generate additional organic flying hours.[25] Of course, no commercial carrier would like a reduction in airlift business. However, whether the reduced incentive has to be compensated depends on whether there has already been significant growth in incentives in recent years as well as on whether the overall incentives even after the reduction are still adequate. On the other hand, flying aircraft less full always costs more. Putting more CPs on a given aircraft will provide less piloting experience despite the current accounting rule that credits all flying hours on a flight to each working CP irrespective of how many working CPs and ACs are on the aircraft.[26] A long-term solution is needed to resolve the recurring problem of inadequate flying hours or piloting experience to meet the aging requirement.

During the 1980s, the aging requirement for a C-141 CP was 40.7 flying hours per month.[27] In recent years, this requirement has declined to 29 hours per month.[28] In the 1980s and 1990s, actual flying hours on average matched the

---

consent from the carrier, AMC will assign the committed aircraft to Stage I, II, or III based on its projected airlift requirements. The entitlements to peacetime business received by a carrier are tied to its level of commitment to Stages I and II. Carriers who want to participate in Stage III only as a patriotic gesture do not earn any guarantee peacetime entitlements but are eligible for overflow business that Stage I and II carriers are unable to provide. (See Carl Evans, *Maintaining Civil Reserve Air Fleet Participation*, Newport, RI: Naval War College, 1993, pp. 13–14.)

CRAF Stage I was activated during Phase I of Operation Desert Shield on August 17, 1990. Stage II was activated at the start of the air campaign on January 17, 1991, and the key parts of the message read: "[T]he Government may exercise its option to increase the services . . . to the full capacity of your aircraft volunteered to CRAF Stage II." (See Mary Chenoweth, *The Civil Reserve Air Fleet and Operation Desert Shield/Desert Storm: Issues for the Future*, MR-298-AF, Santa Monica: RAND, 1993, p. 13.) Actually, only the cargo airlift of Stage II was called up during the deployment phase, because there were very few unfulfilled passenger requirements at the time. Although Stage II could have provided an additional 17 cargo aircraft, many of those aircraft were already flying full time as volunteers, and the net gain was only nine aircraft. The passenger airlift of Stage II was not called up until March 23, 1991, during the redeployment phase, and up to half of the Stage II commitment was expected to be used. (See Ronald Priddy, *A History of the Civil Reserve Air Fleet in Operations Desert Shield, Desert Storm, and Desert Sortie*, Cambridge, MA: Arthur D. Little, Inc., 1993, pp. 146–147 and 176–177.) As to Stage III, it has never been activated.

[25]In this report, a commercial buy is defined as one for international (not domestic) airlift. We focus on international long-distance flights because they are less costly in generating flying hours for strategic airlifters and tankers. There are two types of commercial buys. A fixed buy is made before the beginning of a fiscal year and is not expected to be canceled. An expansion buy is made throughout the fiscal year, when the need arises. If the need disappears, AMC can decide not to issue the buy and incur no penalty.

[26]We will introduce a metric—average number of pilots per flight—to determine whether a pilot is getting less piloting experience during training. If this occurs and starts to affect the quality of training, AMC should refine its aging and proficiency requirements to ensure that pilots receive enough flying hours in piloting.

[27]See Figure A.11 in the appendix.

[28]The reduction from 40.7 to 29 took place over time and in multiple steps. From 1981 to 1990, the number of C-141 aircraft (PAA) held relatively steady, declining from 250 in 1981 to 234 in 1990. Then, C-141s were on their way to retirement and declined sharply from 231 in 1991 to 74 in 1999.

aging requirement. During FY 2000, however, C-141 CPs averaged only 24.1 hours, a level that fell below even the already-reduced requirement of 29 hours. Thus, there were not enough flying hours for aging during that period. Although C-141s are now being retired, insufficient flying will thus delay the promotion of C-141 CPs whether they are flying C-141s or, at a later point, other aircraft.

The aging requirement for a C-17 CP is 35 hours.[29] From 1995 to 1999, the newly deployed C-17 increased its flying hours per CP to about 35, thus meeting the aging requirement. Yet during FY 2000, the number of flying hours per CP dropped to 27.8, well below the aging requirement of 35.

In the 1980s, there were sufficient C-130 flying hours to meet the aging requirement. Yet during the 1990s this number declined, and by FY 2000 the number of flying hours per CP was 24.3—below the requirement of 29 hours per month.[30]

In contrast, the monthly flying hours per KC-135 tanker from 1994 to 1999 stood comfortably above the aging requirement of 25 hours.[31] There was also minimal fluctuation during this period. Although commercial augmentation competes for airlift business with organic airlifters (the C-5, C-141, C-17, and C-130), AMC tankers (the KC-135 and KC-10) face no such competition.[32] This may be one of the reasons KC-135 CPs, unlike those of organic airlifters, flew considerably in excess of their aging requirement. When overall demand was low during FY 2000, however, even KC-135 CPs flew only 24.8 hours per month, slightly below the requirement of 25.

KC-10 CPs flew 5.4 percent more (in monthly flying hours) per year during 1995–1999.[33] Even so, during FY 2000, KC-10 CPs flew 27.9 hours per month, slightly below the aging requirement of 29.

In sum, the CPs of airlifters (the C-5, C-141, C-17, and C-130) and tankers (the KC-135 and KC-10) all had insufficient flying hours during FY 2000.

In the 1990s, AMC needed CPs and ACs to man its sharply decreased fleet of C-141s. In addition to reducing the hiring of C-141 CPs, AMC reduced its monthly flying-hour requirement in order to lengthen the number of years for CPs to be promoted to ACs. This had the effect of reducing the number of ACs and of better matching the lower manning requirement.

[29]See Figure A.12 in the appendix.

[30]See Figure A.13 in the appendix.

[31]See Figure A.14 in the appendix.

[32]The expenses of flying tankers (KC-135s and KC-10s) and the tactical airlifter (C-130s) are not reimbursed by TWCF.

[33]See Figure A.15 in the appendix.

MONTHLY FLYING HOURS PER AIRCRAFT COMMANDER

ACs' flying-hour requirements are significantly less than those of CPs.[34] For example, a CP is required to fly from 1000 to 1400 hours before he can become an AC, but an AC is required to fly only 200 to 500 hours more to become an instructor pilot. An instructor pilot faces no further flying-hour requirement to become a flight examiner.[35] Both CPs and ACs are, however, required to meet their own Pilot Semiannual Flying Requirements (PSFRs).[36] CPs can easily meet these requirements if they fulfill their aging requirement of 25 to 35 hours per month. ACs, by contrast, must first understand PSFRs before they can determine whether these requirements can be easily met. Some of the requirements for C-5 ACs are the number of practices every six months in overseas sorties, takeoffs, landings, instrument approaches, night landings, three-engine miss approaches, and night receiver air refuelings. Many PSFRs can, however, be met in flight simulators. For C-5 ACs, only events such as overseas sorties, Have Quick radio procedures, Secure Voice operations, and some air refueling missions need be performed in an aircraft.[37] Generally, ACs of C-5s or other airlifters or tankers can meet these requirements with monthly flying hours numbering in the teens. In reality, however, the ACs of airlifters and tankers fly considerably more, as a CP must be accompanied by an AC on every flight, and AMC seeks to maintain similar numbers of full-time ACs and CPs in the force. Thus, even during FY 2000, when CPs flew below their aging requirements, ACs had no trouble flying a sufficient amount to meet their PSFRs. Still, it would be of interest to estimate the trend of ACs' flying hours.

Table 2.2 shows monthly flying hours per AC during the past two decades.[38] For the C-5, both the number and the trend of flying hours per month per AC during the 1980s and the 1990s were very similar to those for CPs. The monthly

---

[34]In this sentence, we continue to refer to both ACs and CPs as two pilot categories. The AC pilot category includes the following crew positions: aircraft commander, instructor pilot, and flight examiner. The CP category includes copilot and first pilot.

[35]These are crew positions. The flying-hour requirements to become an AC are 1400, 1300, 1200, and 1000 hours for the C-5, C-141, C-17, and C-130, respectively. The corresponding flying-hour requirements to become an instructor pilot are 300, 300, 200, and 500.

[36]We now return to pilot categories as opposed to crew positions.

[37]ACs are classified into four experience levels: A to D. Regardless of experience level, an AC is required to perform four overseas sorties, two Have Quick radio procedures, and two Secure Voice operations semiannually. ACs must also receive aerial refueling in four, five, six, or seven missions (up to two of which may be in simulators) for experience levels A, B, C, or D, respectively. See *C-5 Aircrew Training*, AFI 11-2C-5, Vol. 1, January 1, 1999.

[38]See also Figures A.16 to A.21 in the appendix.

Table 2.2

Monthly Flying Hours per Aircraft Commander

Aircraft	Data Period (fiscal years)	Average During the 1990s (hours/ month–AC)	Rate of Change (%/year)	*t*-Test Statistic	Level of Significance
C-5	1982–1999	29.1	–0.1	0.4	0.73
C-141	1982–1999	30.3	**–1.6**	**3.5**	**0.00**
C-17	1995–1999	31.1	+4.1	1.5	0.23
C-130	1982–1999	24.6	**–1.1**	**3.4**	**0.01**
KC-135	1994–1999	27.9	–1.1	0.6	0.60
KC-10	1994–1999	28.9	+2.9	1.6	0.21

NOTE: Data points for 1990, 1991, and 1994 were excluded from the determination of the numbers in the third to sixth columns. Bold entries indicate that the probability of a nonzero trend (rate of change) is 95 percent or higher.

flying hours and trends of C-141, C-130, KC-135, and KC-10 ACs were also similar to those of their CPs.[39] During FY 1995 and FY 1996 while C-17s were being introduced into the force, a C-17 AC flew, on average, considerably more than did his CP. Since FY 1997, however, the monthly flying hours per C-17 AC have been similar to those of CPs.

In sum, the ACs of airlifters and tankers had no trouble meeting their PSFRs during the 1980s and 1990s. ACs' flying hours were also similar to those of CPs within every aircraft type.

THE LATEST DATA REINFORCE THE FINDING OF A SHORTAGE

When there is an unexpected shortfall in flying hours during a fiscal year, cutting the expansion buy as opposed to the fixed buy is often preferable because AMC has already made a commitment for fixed buys before the start of the year. During the flying-hour shortage of FY 2000 and FY 2001, AMC cut the cargo rather than the passenger expansion buy (see Figure 2.8) because it does not have organic, dedicated passenger carriers and depends on commercial carriers to transport most passengers.

Figure 2.8 shows that the cargo expansion buy went up in FY 1994 and stayed at a higher level than in 1992 and 1993 until 1999. The question thus arises as to why the increase in cargo buys from 1994 to 1999 did not go to AMC organic assets instead. If it had, the shortage in organic flying hours probably would not have occurred in 2000. In point of fact, the sharp rise in 1994 was due to the

[39]See Figures A.16, A.17, A.19, A.20, and A.21 in the appendix.

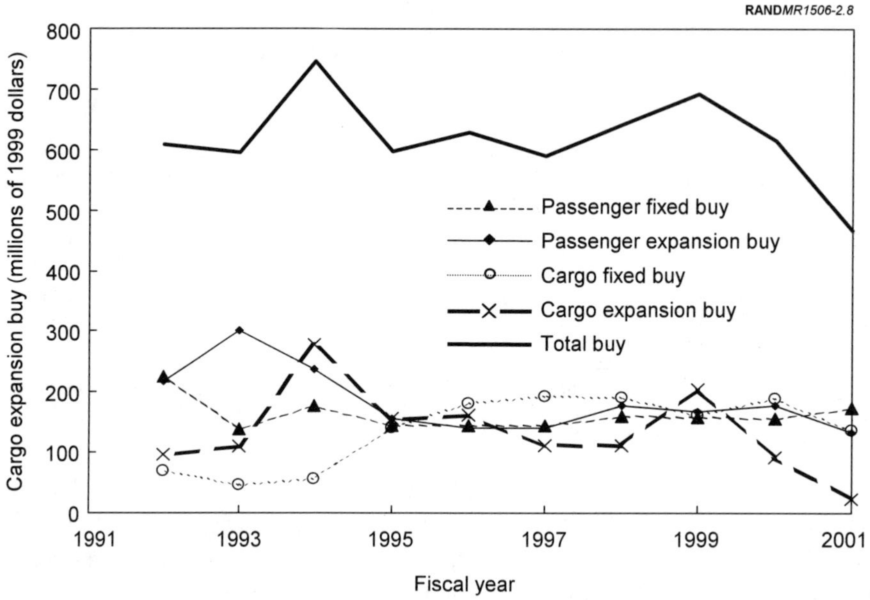

Figure 2.8—AMC Chose to Cut Its Cargo Expansion Buy in FY 2000 and FY 2001

rare occurrence of weep-hole cracks in C-141 wings.[40] As shown in Figures 2.3 and 2.5, both total strategic airlifter and C-141 flying levels were below normal during 1994, and AMC used commercial expansion buys to fill the gap. This was consistent with AMC's traditional approach toward meeting flying demand: Each year, AMC prefers to fly the number of hours that meets the pilot training requirement, and if demand exceeds that number, it prefers to contract commercial fixed and expansion buys rather than to fly more itself. As shown in Figures 2.7 and A.11, C-5 and C-141 CPs were already flying in excess of their flying requirements during 1995–1999.[41] AMC thus turned to the commercial air carriers during that period to meet the excess flying demand.

Figure 2.9 takes a closer look at the cut in the cargo expansion buy depicted in Figure 2.8.[42] A sharp cut occurred in July 2000, and the cut continued to the point at which the buy was near zero by the early months of calendar year 2001.

[40]The wing-crack problem was described earlier in this chapter.

[41]The only exception was the C-5 during 1995. C-17s are not included here because during the same period, C-17s were still in the buildup phase and could not fly more.

[42]We have included the combination buy (a mix of cargo and passenger buys) in the cargo as opposed to passenger buy because AMC does so in tallying the total cargo expansion buy.

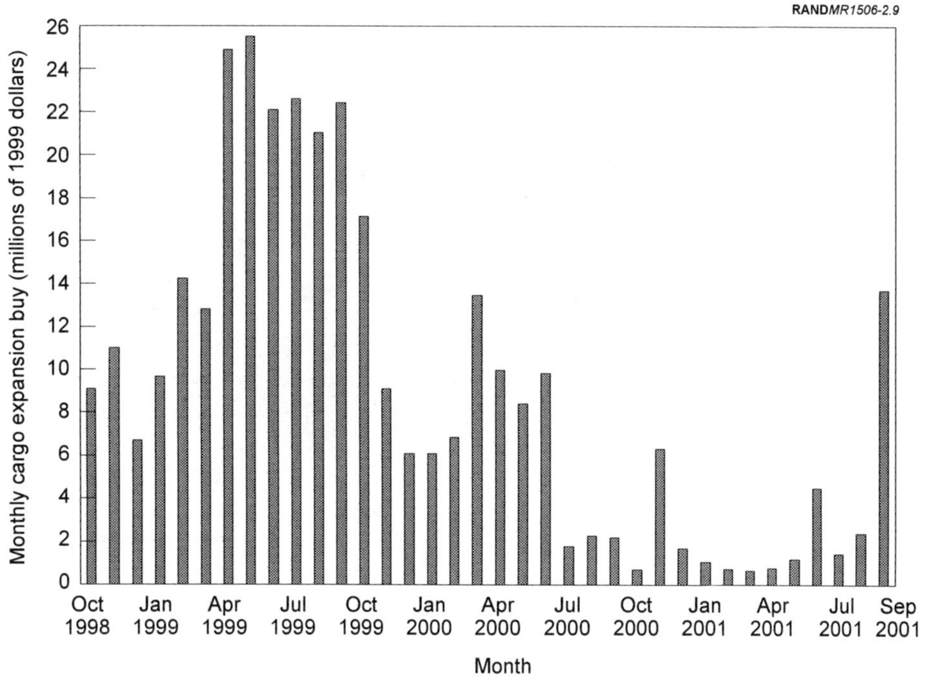

Figure 2.9—The Cargo Expansion Buy Declined Sharply in July 2000 Until August 2001

It then remained low until activities surged after September 11.[43] Unfortunately, even with such a large cut in the cargo expansion buy, CPs for all airlifters and tankers still failed to meet their monthly flying-hour requirement during FY 2000 and FY 2001.

In point of fact, in the face of the flying-hour shortage during FY 2000 and the first half of FY 2001, AMC tried to increase organic flying during the second half of FY 2001 (see Figure 2.10).[44] The average monthly flying hours per CP for airlifters during the second half of FY 2001 thus increased from 16 percent to 23 percent over those during the first half of that fiscal year.[45] While these efforts did not eliminate the shortage, they did reduce it considerably. For example,

[43]Figure 2.9 shows the surge in the cargo expansion buy during September 2001, at which time it was close to $14 million, or about $12 million above normal. In contrast, the cargo fixed buy stayed at $12 million in September 2001 and changed little from prior months. This is to be expected because the fixed buy is contracted at the beginning of the fiscal year, whereas the expansion buy is contracted much closer to the time of need and is designed to meet unexpected demand.

[44]See Chapter Eight for details.

[45]In contrast, the monthly flying hours per pilot during the second half of FY 2000 showed a decline from the first half (see Figure 2.10).

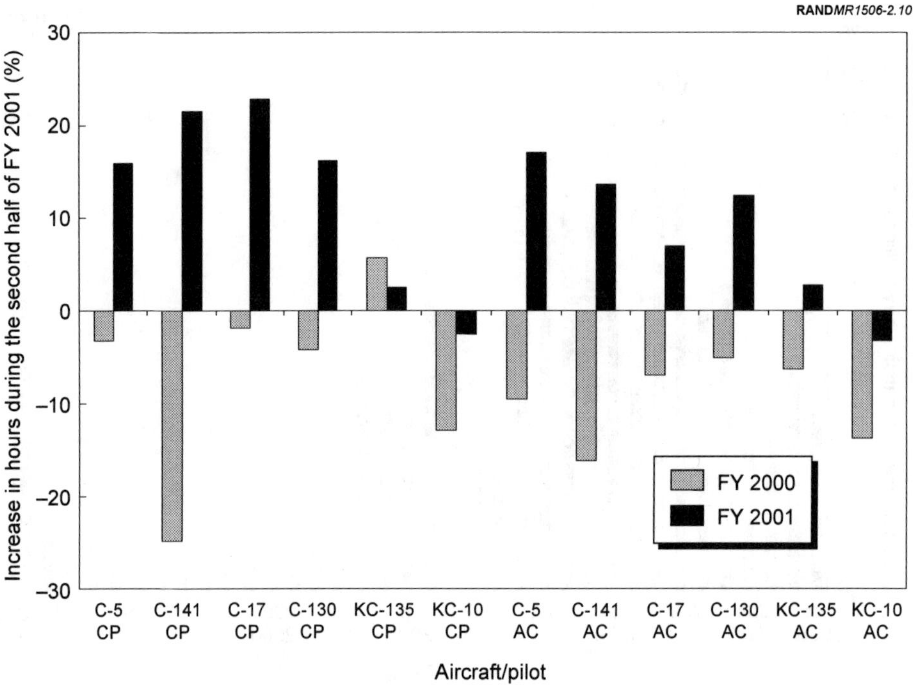

Figure 2.10—AMC Increased Monthly Flying Hours per Pilot During the Second Half of FY 2001

Table 2.3

AMC Was Able to Reduce but Not Eliminate the Flying-Hour Shortage[a]

	Monthly Flying Hours per Pilot				
	Full Year FY 2001	First Half FY 2001	Full Year FY 2000	Full Year FY 1999	Aging Requirement
Copilots					
C-5	**28.3**	**26.2**	**26.0**	30.5	30
C-141	**24.9**	**22.6**	**24.1**	33.4	29
C-17	**32.0**	**28.7**	**27.8**	**33.6**	35
C-130	**21.2**	**19.6**	**24.3**	**25.5**	29
KC-135	**23.5**	**23.2**	**24.8**	30.1	25
KC-10	**22.1**	**22.4**	**27.9**	35.5	29
Aircraft commanders					
C-5	22.4	20.7	24.3	26.9	NA[b]
C-141	24.0	22.7	24.7	31.1	NA
C-17	29.2	28.1	28.3	33.6	NA
C-130	21.8	20.6	21.6	24.2	NA
KC-135	20.7	20.4	22.0	27.8	NA
KC-10	21.2	21.6	26.0	31.7	NA

[a]Bold entries indicate failure to meet aging requirement.

[b]Not applicable.

such efforts brought the monthly hours per C-5 CP up from 26.2 during the first half to 30.4 during the second half of FY 2001, resulting in an average of 28.3 hours for the full year (see Table 2.3). However, this average was still 1.7 hours short of the required 30 hours per month per CP. C-141 CPs were on their part 4.1 hours short; C-17 CPs, 3 hours; C-130 CPs, 7.8 hours; KC-135 CPs, 1.5 hours; and KC-10 CPs, 6.9 hours. Shortfalls will recur from time to time because one cannot know when and how many peacetime deployments will occur in any given year.[46] On the other hand, ACs do not have an aging requirement, and monthly flying hours numbering in the teens will satisfy their proficiency requirement. Although ACs flew less during FY 2000 and FY 2001 than during FY 1999, they still had no trouble meeting their proficiency requirement.

ENGAGEMENT VERSUS READINESS MISSIONS

As shown in the previous two sections, AMC pilots did not fly more in the 1990s than in the 1980s. However, they may still be flying more short-notice missions as opposed to routine missions with advance notice. Yet it is harder and more costly for AMC to assemble the necessary aircraft and personnel for short-notice missions, and pilots prefer not to fly missions with little advance notice.

If such missions are occurring more frequently, AMC might either have to endure the situation or contract more of them to commercial carriers.

The AMC Flying-Hour Program divides missions into two groups: O&M and TWCF.[47] O&M missions are not reimbursed by customers, but TWCF missions are. O&M missions are further divided into test, training, and ferry (TTF) and joint airdrop/air transportability training (JA/ATT). TWCF missions are divided into channel, exercise, contingency, and SAAMs. Channel missions are scheduled deliveries between established aerial ports of embarkation (APOEs) and aerial ports of debarkation (APODs). The other TWCF missions are generally unscheduled, have shorter notice,[48] and deliver passengers and cargo to support joint exercises, small-scale contingencies, humanitarian relief operations,

---

[46]The OEF has significantly increased AMC flying hours. However, OEF is considered a contingency with a high air mobility demand, not a peacetime operation. In any case, it will eventually end. Nor does one know at what level U.S. counterterrorism efforts as a whole will be sustained and for how long. AMC cannot count on these continuous, heightened activities to solve the flying-hour shortage.

[47]The TWCF is "(t)hat part of the Defense Business Operations fund operated by AMC to finance the operating costs of the airlift services provided by AMC, who is reimbursed for such costs by authorized customers to whom airlift services are rendered. Formerly known as DBOF-T." See *Command Data Book*, November 1999, p. 144.

[48]It is possible that as contingencies mature and as schedules become set, missions are no longer short notice. Unfortunately, AMC has not used a classification that separates short-notice from long-notice missions. Nor is "short notice" defined. One can still say, however, that other TWCF missions, on average, have shorter notice than channel missions.

presidential travel, and the like. Pilots prefer channel missions because they are scheduled well in advance, so pilots are not called out of town unexpectedly. AMC management prefers such missions as well because it can reliably and accurately schedule pilots to fly them to satisfy aging and proficiency requirements. AMC also knows that many training elements will be accomplished in channel missions. We believe, however, that short-notice missions can be used to train pilots for short-notice wartime missions.

We have classified missions into three categories: channel, engagement, and O&M. Channel missions are TWCF missions that AMC favors for maintaining and upgrading pilots' flying skills. Engagement missions consist of the other TWCF missions that AMC is expected to perform to support U.S. peacetime operations.[49] O&M missions refer to those that are not reimbursed by customers or are dedicated to training (without airlifting items for customers at the same time). Flying hours for missions in any of these three categories can be used to satisfy pilots' flying-hour requirements. The military annual flying-hours for the airlifters (the C-5, C-141, C-17, and C-130) during peacetime declined 63 percent between 1981 and 2000 (see Figure 2.11).

When we compared the annual engagement missions conducted during 1981 and 1989, we found an increase of 35,000 flying hours, or 32 percent. Conversely, we found annual channel missions to have declined by 57,000 hours, or 27 percent, and O&M by 24,000 hours, or 15 percent.[50]

It is instructive to see how AMC managed airlift demand and supply during 1981–1989. When the engagement demand rose, AMC used its own assets to

---

[49]Paul Killingsworth classifies peacetime missions into two categories: engagement and readiness. The former has high priority and short notice and is composed of small-scale contingencies, expeditionary Air Force support, banner operations (presidential support), humanitarian relief operations, short-notice SAAMs, and mission support. The latter has lower priority and advance planning and consists of local training, exercises, JA/ATT, channels, long-lead SAAMs, and efforts such as air evacuations. (Information is derived from a private communication with the author in January 2001.) We do not use Killingsworth's mission categories here for two reasons. First, the data in the authoritative Flying-Hour Program cannot be readily reclassified into these two categories. Second, missions in Killingsworth's engagement category, like the channel missions in his readiness category, can be used to meet flying-hour requirements, which can be considered readiness requirements. In this important sense, Killingsworth's engagement missions are not distinctive from his readiness missions. In any case, our O&M and channel missions combined should approximate Killingsworth's readiness category, while our engagement missions should be similar to his engagement category.

[50]See Figure A.22 in the appendix. To understand why engagement flying hours increased, one would have to examine and tally the numerous activities every year during those years. For example, the rise in engagement missions in FY 1984 was caused by several major events (on top of other more typical engagement activities): the U.S. intervention in Grenada from October 25 to November 19, 1983; airlift missions conducted in association with U.S. Airborne Warning and Control System (AWACS) aircraft deployment to help Egyptians monitor Libyan threats to their country, from March 19 to April 9, 1984; President Reagan's trip to China from April 7 to May 2, 1984; and the deployment of U.S. minesweeping assets to the Red Sea from August 7 to October 2, 1984.

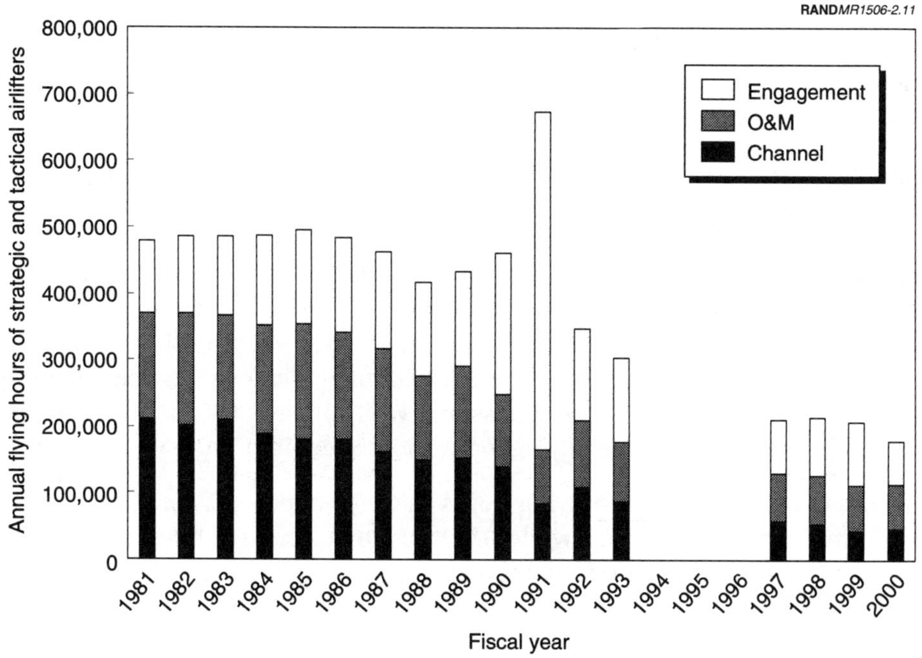

NOTE: The years 1990 and 1991 were not considered peacetime in this study.

Figure 2.11—Military Airlifters' Annual Flying Hours During Peacetime Declined After the Cold War

perform these activities, as it would do traditionally. At the same time, AMC preferred to fly just enough hours to meet its pilots' training requirements. Therefore, when AMC pilots flew more engagement missions than expected, AMC reduced the organic flying of channel missions, which indeed happened during this period. The question remains, however, as to why the 57,000-hour decrease in channel missions exceeded the 35,000-hour increase in engagement missions. This was because C-5, C-141, and C-130 CPs generally flew in excess of their requirements during 1981–1989 even with the larger reduction.[51] In other words, if AMC had reduced channel as well as O&M flying any less, its pilots would have had to fly even more than they were required. Our recommendations[52] for alleviating flying-hour shortages follow AMC's approach of favoring organic assets to fly engagement missions and using commercial ser-

[51]See Figure 2.7 and Figures A.11 and A.13 in the appendix.

[52]This will be discussed in Chapter Eight.

vices as shock absorbers[53] while also focusing on creating new avenues for AMC to fly more when it needs to. Channel flying also declined faster than engagement and O&M over the past two decades.[54] This trend can be unfavorable for AMC given its preference for using channel flying for pilot training.

Figure 2.12 shows the three mission categories for the C-5. During the past two decades, O&M missions remained stable at about 20 percent of C-5 pilots' flying hours. On the other hand, channel missions steadily declined at a rate of 5.6 percent per year, and engagement missions rose by 13 percent per year. By 1999, annual engagement missions constituted 68 percent of the total missions flown on a flying-hour basis, compared to only 11 percent in 1981. In the 1980s, in other words, the annual flying hours for channel missions were significantly higher than those for engagement missions, while in the 1990s the situation was reversed. C-5 pilots had been flying many more short-notice missions.

For the C-141, the shares of flying hours in the channel-mission category declined by 2.5 percent per year, while O&M missions increased by 2.7 percent per year and engagement missions increased by 2.1 percent per year.[55] C-141 channel missions and engagement missions showed trends similar to those of the C-5, but with less intensity. Thus, a similar concern arises that the C-141 is bearing an increasing portion of short-notice missions.

The trend lines also reflect the penetration of the new C-17 during the second half of the 1990s.[56] These trends do not reflect how the mission percentages changed for a matured airlifter such as the C-5 or C-141. The end points (in 1999) may be more illustrative of future trends for a maturing C-17. In 1999, channel missions accounted for 31 percent of all annual flying hours, O&M for 23 percent, and engagement missions for 46 percent. As with the C-5 and C-141, engagement missions accounted for the largest share of AMC's C-17 peacetime flying hours. It should be emphasized, however, that there are too few data points to justify any definitive statements about C-17 trends.

The O&M share of C-130 flying hours was stable and accounted for about half of all flying hours.[57] Channel missions showed a steady decline of 4.5 percent per year, while engagement missions exhibited an increase of 4 percent per year.

---

[53]They are shock absorbers because AMC will use commercial air carriers to take care of the excess when there is an unexpected airlift demand. Likewise, when there is a deficit in demand, commercial services will be cut to allow more flying hours for AMC's own pilots.

[54]See Figure A.22 in the appendix.

[55]See Figure A.23 in the appendix.

[56]See Figure A.24 in the appendix.

[57]See Figure A.25 in the appendix.

In sum, for all four airlifters (the C-5, C-141, C-17, and C-130), engagement missions accounted for a growing share of flying hours. Moreover, for the C-5, C-141, and C-130, channel missions, which are favored by AMC management and pilots, declined. The O&M shares of flying hours for the C-5, C-141, and C-130 remained relatively stable over the past two decades. We do not have data on the KC-135 and KC-10 tankers with which to address trends in various mission categories.

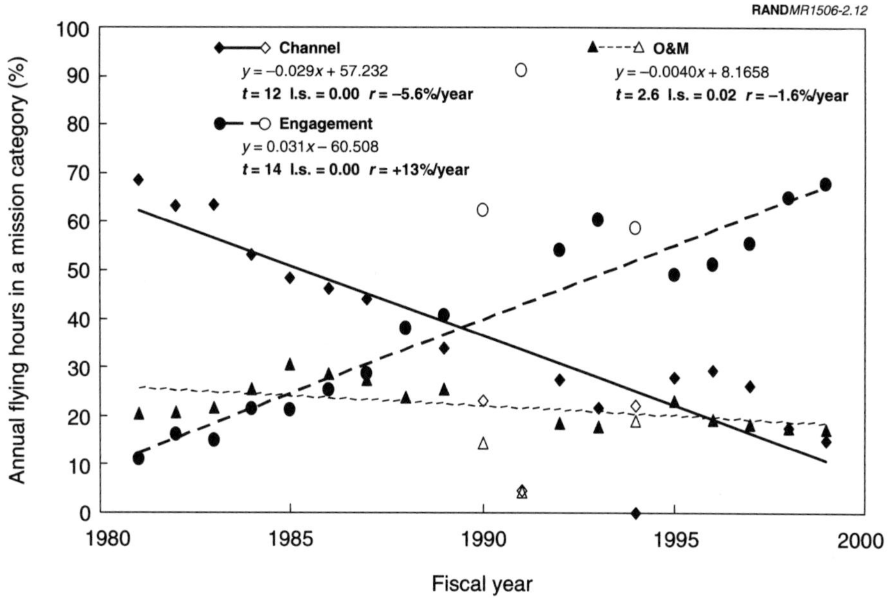

NOTE: Data points for 1990, 1991, and 1994 were excluded from the determination of the trend lines.

Figure 2.12—C-5: Growing Engagement Missions and Declining Channel Missions

Chapter Three

DO ACTUAL NUMBERS OF COPILOTS AND AIRCRAFT COMMANDERS DEVIATE FROM THOSE AUTHORIZED?

This chapter examines two issues. First, does AMC have more CPs and ACs than are authorized? If this is consistently the case, AMC should provide a justification for the excess or be prepared to make adjustments in pilots' duties and workloads in the event that a cut comes. Second, how does the actual CP/AC ratio deviate from that authorized? If the deviation persists but is justified, DoD should try to convince Congress not to authorize specific numbers of CPs and ACs. Instead, Congress should focus on the overall budget, leaving AMC to optimize the mix of CPs and ACs.

NUMBERS OF COPILOTS AND AIRCRAFT COMMANDERS

Each year, Congress authorizes specific numbers of full-time CPs and ACs to man AMC's air mobility operations. A key determinant of an authorized number is the crew ratio, which, for a given aircraft type, is the average number of pilots required to man an aircraft. The authorized numbers often contrast with the actual numbers of CPs and ACs at AMC.

Figure 3.1 shows three ratios of actual to authorized personnel. The CP ratio is the actual number of CPs in relation to those authorized for all airlifters and tankers (C-5s, C-141s, C-17s, C-130s, KC-135s, and KC-10s). The AC ratio is the actual number of ACs in relation to authorized ones. The CP + AC ratio is the actual number of CPs and ACs in relation to the authorized number. During 1982–2001, the average CP ratio increased 1 percent per year. In the 1980s, the CP ratio was less than one, but in the 1990s it fluctuated widely both above and below one.[1] In theory, the more the ratio exceeds one, the more difficult it can be for AMC to hire more CPs if existing CPs are found to be overworked, as

[1]We will discuss the wide fluctuation in the number of CPs during the 1990s later in this chapter.

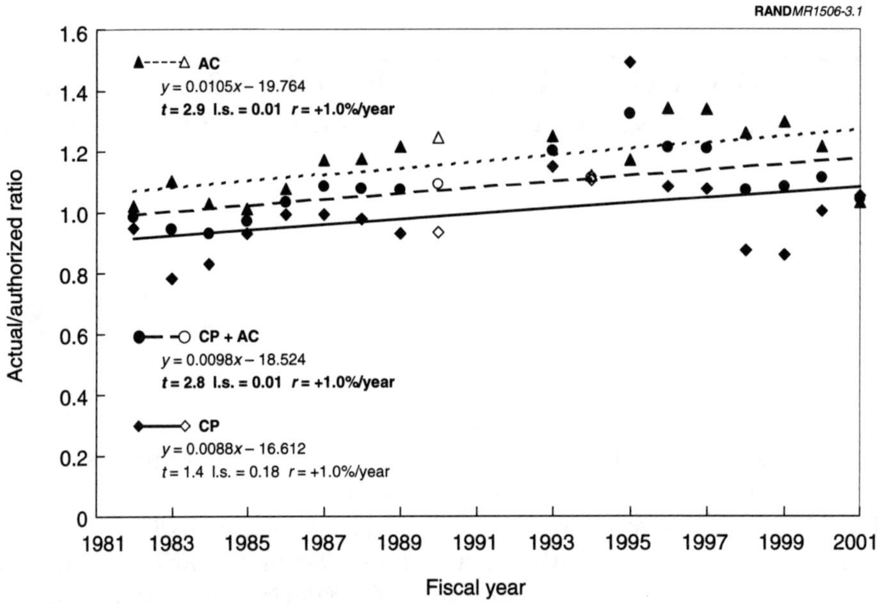

NOTE: Data points for 1990 and 1994 were excluded from the determination of the trend lines.

Figure 3.1—Actual and Authorized Ratios for All Airlifters and Tankers

Congress can argue that the current number of CPs already well exceeds what has been authorized. In this sense, an upward trend is unfavorable. In practice, however, the actual numbers of CPs and ACs did deviate for years from those authorized. Apparently, Congress recognized the difficulties AMC would have in matching the authorized numbers as well as the negative implications of enforcing this match.[2] On the other hand, the actual number of CPs dropped to only 0.1 percent above that authorized by FY 2000 and was only 5 percent above that authorized in FY 2001.

The AC data show that even in the 1980s, the ratio of actual to authorized ACs exceeded one. Indeed, from 1982 to 2001, there was an uptrend of 1.0 percent per year to the point at which the actual number of ACs was 22 percent above that authorized by FY 2000. During FY 2001, however, this number dropped abruptly to only 3 percent above that authorized.

---

[2]For example, increasing the number of CPs and reducing the number of ACs to match those authorized would increase the flying hours for pilot training. Additional flying hours would be very costly whenever AMC faced flying-hour shortages.

The CP + AC data show that the ratio of actual to authorized CPs and ACs had been above one since 1986, having trended upward at a rate of 1 percent per year from 1982 to 2001. By FY 2000, the actual number of CPs and ACs was 11 percent above that authorized. During FY 2001, it was only 4 percent above.

In sum, during the past two decades, the actual numbers of CPs and ACs increased. During FY 2001, however, those numbers were only 3 percent to 5 percent above what Congress had authorized.

COPILOT-TO-AIRCRAFT COMMANDER RATIOS

Even if the actual total number of CPs and ACs is equal to that authorized, the mix of CPs and ACs—or the actual CP/AC ratio—may still differ from that authorized.

Each airlifter or tanker flight requires at least two pilots. The salary cost of a flight would be lowest if there were precisely two pilots: one CP and one AC. The ratio of full-time CPs to ACs serving at AMC airlift and air refueling wings would then be one, as CPs and ACs would fly similar number of hours per year.[3] A higher ratio (more CPs than ACs) could lead to an insufficient number of ACs for commanding flights. On the other hand, a relative surplus of ACs over CPs would result in a higher salary cost, as ACs are paid annually an average of \$15,000 more than CPs.[4] In the face of a flying-hour shortage, however, there is a much higher cost associated with generating additional flying hours. For example, the monthly flying-hour requirement for a C-17 CP is 35,[5] whereas that for an AC is only in the teens. If AMC replaced a C-17 AC with a CP, each additional flying hour per month (or 12 hours per year) for a CP would have a marginal (or variable) flying cost of \$30,000.[6] Because it is likely that the replacement would require much more than one hour per month, the flying cost would be much higher than the salary savings.[7] In sum, when AMC is short of

[3]Because this study focuses on AMC pilots who perform full-time flying duties, we exclude pilots at AMC headquarters or wing units who perform mostly administrative duties.

[4]This is based on the annual regular military compensation for ACs and CPs. See Chapter Seven for more detail.

[5]See Table 2.3 for a C-17 CP's aging requirement as well as those for other aircraft types.

[6]We used the variable cost per aircraft flying hour listed in the *Command Data Book*, November 1999, p. 77. As shown in Chapter Four, the average number of pilots on each flight of a strategic airlifter is about three, while that of a tactical airlifter is two. For each of the extra C-17 flights here, we assume the aircrew to be composed of two CPs and one AC, and thus each hour of aircraft flight generates two CP flying hours. We divide the C-17 aircraft flying-hour cost of \$61,000 by two to get the C-17 CP flying-hour cost of \$30,000. The corresponding CP flying-hour costs for the C-5 and C-141 are \$54,000 and \$21,000.

[7]This is the case not only for the C-17 but also for other airlifters and tankers. For all cases, we have assumed that the extra flight is dedicated to training and is not reimbursed for expenses. It is possible that AMC reduces commercial buys and uses these extra organic flights to carry the same cargo

flying hours, changing the mix to include more CPs would actually increase its net cost, at least in the short term.

In reality, many flights require more than two pilots. For example, while an airlift aircrew is normally limited to 16 hours of operations per day (for flying and pre- and postmission activities), this limit was raised during the Gulf War to 18 hours per day. Moreover, with an additional pilot or an augmented crew, crew duty time is allowed to increase to 24 hours per day. Indeed, it is not uncommon for augmented flights to account for as much as half or even two-thirds of all strategic airlifter flights. Special operations flights, which are more complex and often take place at night, require three pilots regardless of flight time.[8] Unlike augmented flights, however, special operations flights account for only a small percentage of all flights. Adjusting for the extra pilots needed for these augmented and special operations flights as well as for other considerations, Congress, with inputs from the Air Force, authorizes specific numbers of full-time CPs and ACs at AMC every year.

Shifts in the pace of recruitment, promotion, transfer, resignation, and retirement in AMC cause the actual ratio of CPs to ACs in any given year to differ from that authorized.[9] When the actual ratio deviates significantly from that authorized, concerns can arise that Congress' authorization is not being met. Fortunately, Congress generally does not enforce the ratio that it authorizes.

Figure 3.2 shows the two CP/AC ratios (actual and authorized) for the C-5. In the 1980s, the negative deviation of actual from authorized figures showed that there were too few CPs relative to ACs, if congressional authorization were used as a reference. Immediately after the demise of the Soviet Union, the U.S. Air Force began to reduce its number of fighter pilots. To counteract the decrease in pilot positions in the Air Combat Command, AMC accepted more pilots graduating from Undergraduate Pilot Training (UPT) for airlift missions. Consequently, the number of CPs (and thus the actual ratio) surged during 1992–1995.[10] Fortunately, AMC quickly processed the excess CPs through the aging program. As these CPs turned into ACs, the actual ratio dropped signifi-

---

and passengers originally intended for commercial flights. Even then, AMC might have to pay some kind of penalty or fee to maintain enough incentives for CRAF participants. The extra flying cost, which is typically for many additional hours per month per replacement (replacing an AC with a CP), would easily overwhelm the salary savings.

[8]The C-5, C-141, and C-17, but not the C-130, are used for special operations.

[9]The actual ratio can also be called the assigned ratio because AMC calls the actual numbers of CPs and ACs the "assigned numbers."

[10]The number of CPs in AMC surged from 112 in FY 1990 to a peak of 276 in FY 1995, while the number of ACs dropped from 169 to 146 in the same time frame.

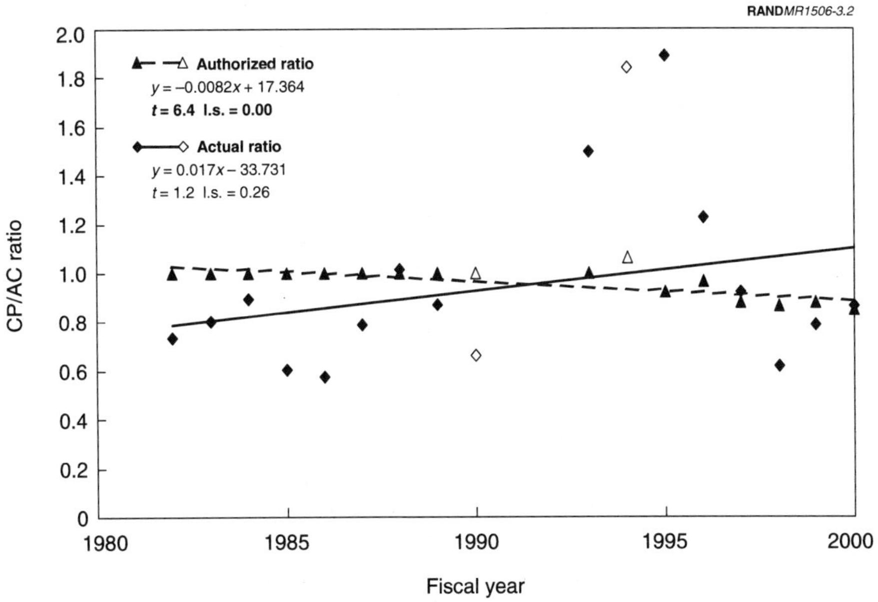

NOTE: Data points for 1990 and 1994 were excluded from the determination of the trend lines.

Figure 3.2—C-5: Actual and Authorized CP/AC Ratios

cantly, even falling below the authorized ratio by 1998. By 2000, the actual ratio was 2 percent over that authorized.[11] However, by 2001 the actual ratio was 31 percent above that authorized.[12] Thus, the actual ratio for the C-5 can deviate widely from that authorized from one year to the next.

The actual ratio for the C-141 dropped significantly further below the authorized ratio in the 1990s than in the 1980s.[13] During FY 2000, however, the actual ratio increased while the authorized ratio dropped significantly, bringing the two ratios much closer together. In FY 2001, the actual ratio was very close to the authorized value, showing only a 2 percent deviation above that value.

The actual ratio for the C-17 rapidly approached the authorized ratio through 2000. By 2001, the actual ratio was 35 percent above that authorized.

---

[11]Because it is difficult to hit the target exactly, a difference of a few percentage points can be interpreted as matching the authorized number.

[12]In March 2002, Craig Vara at AMC/DOT provided us with data for FY 2001. These points (not plotted in Figures 3.2 and A.26 to A.30) are included in the discussion in the text.

[13]See Figures A.26 to A.30 in the appendix for the C-141, C-17, C-130, KC-135, and KC-10.

The actual ratio for the C-130 had long been considerably below the authorized ratio. In the late 1990s, the deviation was about 30 percent. Since the authorized ratio is near unity, there were 30 pecent fewer CPs than ACs, if the authorized ratio is used as a guide. In FY 2001, the actual ratio rose from well below the authorized ratio to 19 percent above it.

The actual ratio for the KC-135 tanker was significantly below that authorized (30 percent to 40 percent) during 1996–2000. The actual ratio for the other tanker, the KC-10, deviated from the authorized ratio by an even larger amount—40 percent to 50 percent—during the same period. For 2001, the actual ratio for the KC-135 was only 15 percent below the authorized ratio, but that of the KC-10 was still 42 percent below.

In sum, the actual CP/AC ratio can fluctuate widely and deviate substantially from that authorized. During 2001, the actual ratios for all four airlifters (the C-5, C-141, C-17, and C-130) were above those authorized, while those for the two tankers (the KC-135 and KC-10) continued to fall well below their authorized numbers. In the context of a flying-hour shortage, however, it would be costly to replace ACs with CPs because the latter must fly more than ACs, yielding an extra flying cost much higher than the salary savings. Therefore, the key result in this section is not so much that the deviations in the numbers and ratios of CPs and ACs have been identified but rather that the authorized, not the actual, numbers should sometimes be adjusted. Otherwise, the cost of complying with the authorized ratio could be costly, with the extra flying cost far exceeding any salary savings achieved.

Chapter Four

DO PILOTS SPEND LESS TIME IN PILOTING?

The current AMC accounting rule for meeting aging and proficiency requirements is that each working CP aboard a flight receives credit for all the flying hours in that flight regardless of the number of pilots in the aircrew. The implication is that one hour spent piloting an aircraft and one hour spent observing another individual piloting that aircraft are equivalent for the purposes of meeting the flying-hour requirement.[1] In reality, however, piloting provides better training than does observing. This chapter assesses the trend in time pilots spend piloting as opposed to observing.

Craig Vara at AMC/DOT provided us with the numbers of full-time CPs and ACs for a given type of airlifter or tanker. He also provided average monthly flying hours per CP and per AC. On the basis of his data, we calculated the total annual pilot flying hours flown by full-time CPs and ACs for each aircraft type.[2] Separately, we obtained the corresponding total annual aircraft flying hours by subtracting those aircraft flying hours flown by associate reservists from AMC aircraft flying hours.[3] We then divided the total annual pilot flying hours by the total annual aircraft flying hours to determine the average number of pilots (CPs plus ACs) per flight. We similarly calculated the average number of CPs per flight and the average number of ACs per flight. The sum of these two numbers equals the average number of pilots per flight.

---

[1]AMC already keeps a separate record of in-seat and other flying hours. "In-seat flying hours" are those that accrue when the pilot is in a pilot seat. "Other flying hours" are those that are accumulated when the pilot is not in a pilot seat. When a pilot is in a pilot seat, we define his activities as piloting. Even when the aircraft is flying on autopilot, the two pilots in pilot seats will still have much to do—e.g., monitoring the flight management system and maintaining communications, including sending and receiving messages.

[2]Note the difference between pilot flying hours and aircraft flying hours. If a flight crew consists of three pilots, each aircraft flying hour would generate three pilot flying hours.

[3]Recall that associate reserve units do not have their own aircraft, and their associate reservists fly organic assets.

Figure 4.1 shows all three measures for the C-5. The number of ACs per flight approximated 1.5 over the past two decades. Because every flight must be commanded by an AC, unity is the minimum number for this measure. Unity also provides the most flying opportunity for CPs to satisfy their aging requirement according to the current AMC counting rule. Thus, reducing the number from 1.5 to 1.0 will provide more flying hours to CPs, thereby helping reduce CPs' flying-hour shortage. Figure 4.1 also shows that during the last two decades, the number of CPs per flight increased from around 1.0 to roughly 1.5.

The minimum number of pilots (CPs and ACs) for a regular C-5 flight is 2.0, but 3.0 for extended and special operations flights. Thus, averaging over all C-5 flights, the minimum number of pilots is somewhere between 2.0 and 3.0. The actual number of pilots per flight increased from 2.5 in the early 1980s to as high as 3.5 or 4.0 during 1995–1997 and declined to slightly below 3.0 by 1999. The high number during 1995–1997 resulted from the previously discussed surge in the number of CPs—which stemmed in turn from a surplus of UPT graduates and from the need to provide such graduates with aging flying hours. Assigning more pilots to a flight than is strictly required could affect the quality of training. Fortunately, this problem has diminished as the average number has declined to below 3.0. Still, the general upward trend from 2.5 in the early 1980s to

RANDMR1506-4.1

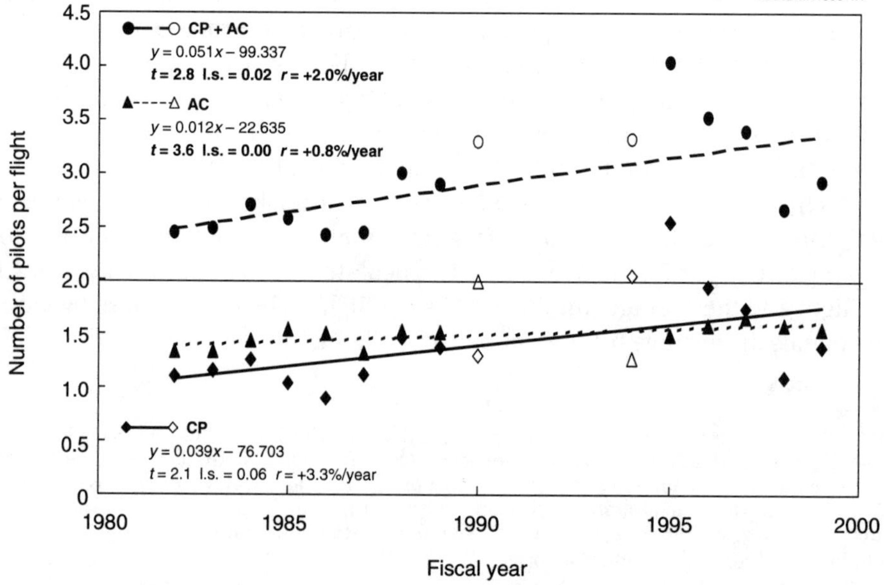

NOTE: Data points for 1990 and 1994 were excluded from the determination of the trend lines.

Figure 4.1—C-5 Average Number of Pilots per Flight

3.0 by the late 1990s could be a warning sign pointing to a reduction in flexibility. When pilots need more flying hours to meet their requirements, one cannot simply place additional pilots on a flight without negatively affecting their training. It is, however, possible to replace an AC with a CP if the flight originally planned to have two ACs on board.

Figure 4.2 shows three average-pilots-per-flight measures for the C-141. The average number of ACs per flight increased from 1.0 in the 1980s and early 1990s to close to 2.0 in the late 1990s. This reflects the excess of ACs over CPs in the C-141 force as the fleet is retired. The overall average number of pilots per flight increased from 2.0 in the 1980s to 3.0 in the latter half of the 1990s. Although C-141s will soon be completely retired, the increasing numbers of pilots per C-141 flight may still be a concern because many of these pilots will be transferred to fly other AMC aircraft types. If such pilots do not soon receive adequate training, flying safety could be compromised both now and in the future. The average-pilots-per-flight figures for the C-17 are shown in Figure 4.3. The few data points for this newly introduced aircraft indicate 1.5 CPs and

RANDMR1506-4.2

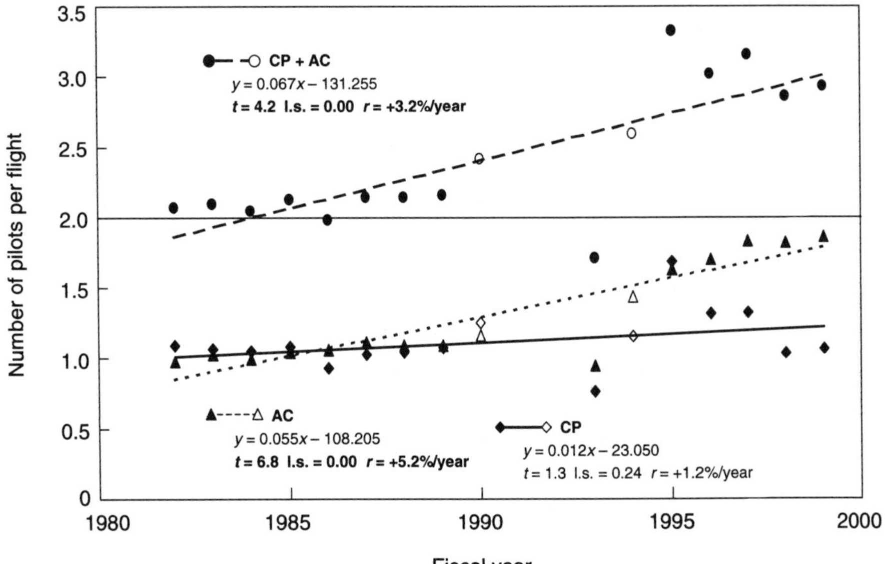

NOTE: Data points for 1990 and 1994 were excluded from the determination of the trend lines.

Figure 4.2—C-141 Average Number of Pilots per Flight

RANDMR1506-4.3

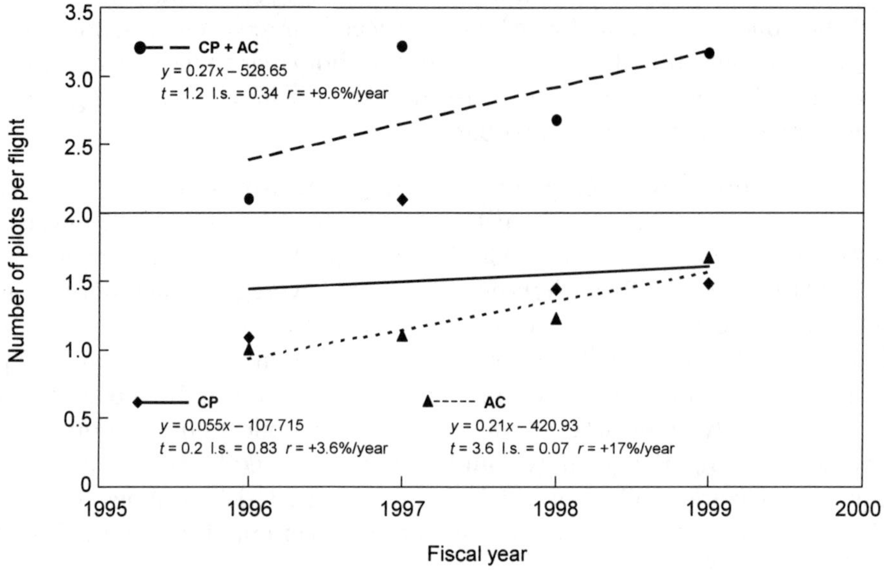

Figure 4.3—C-17 Average Number of Pilots per Flight

1.7 ACs per flight by 1999. An average number above 3.0 signifies that more pilots are placed on these flights than are technically needed.[4]

The average-pilots-per-flight figures for the C-130 are shown in Figure 4.4. The average number of pilots per flight trended slightly upward toward 2.0 by the late 1990s. Unlike the strategic airlifters (the C-5, C-141, and C-17), the C-130 is a tactical airlifter. Its flight times are short enough that it does not require a third pilot as an augmented crew member. That the average number is close to the minimum number of 2.0 implies that the practice is to place two but not three pilots on a C-130 flight.[5] Thus, C-130 pilots are trained and aged in 100 percent piloting and 0 percent observing, unlike the case for strategic airlifter pilots, who are trained on a mix of the two. We do not have data for the two tankers, the KC-135 and KC-10.

In sum, the average numbers of pilots per flight for the strategic airlifters (the C-5, C-141, and C-17) trended upward toward a figure of 3.0 or above. Such a

---

[4]The C-17 requires two pilots to man a normal-length flight and three pilots to man an extended or special operations flight.

[5]Because a C-130 flight requires at least two pilots, it comes as a surprise that the average number, especially during the 1980s, dropped below two. We have not included those few occasions when staff pilots (not full-time pilots) have joined the flight crew. The focus here is on the flying hours of full-time CPs and ACs. We do not count the flying hours of staff pilots.

RANDMR1506-4.4

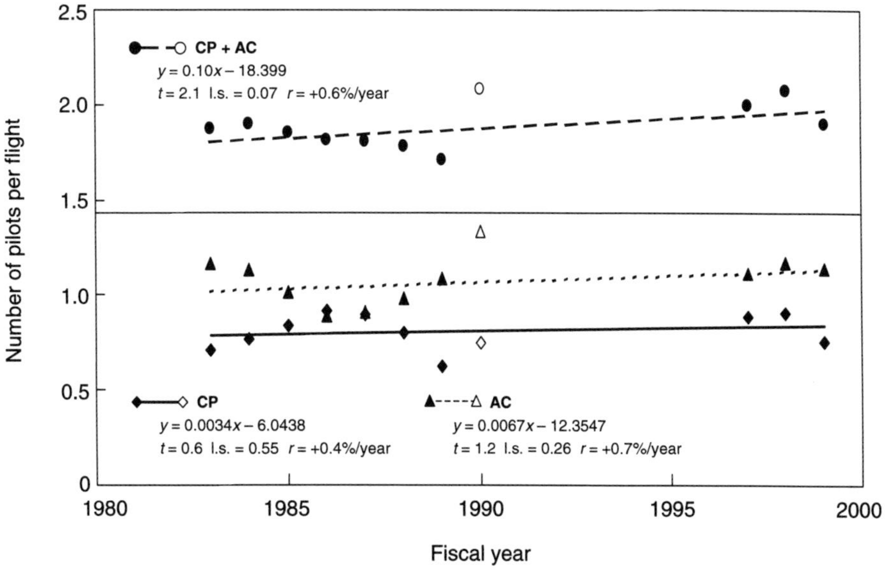

NOTE: Data points for 1990 were excluded from the determination of the trend lines.

Figure 4.4—C-130 Average Number of Pilots per Flight

high number means that if pilots need more flying hours in the future, providing those flying hours by placing extra pilots on each flight will increase the ratio of observing-pilot time, with potentially negative consequences for the quality of training. On the other hand, the average number of ACs per flight for these strategic airlifters has remained at 1.5 or more in recent years. Therefore, when CPs need more flying hours, an option exists to replace the extra (second) AC with a CP on a flight. As for the C-130 tactical airlifter, the practice of placing no more than two pilots on a flight implies that such pilots are spending all their time piloting as opposed to observing during the flight. This arrangement yields the best training quality.

Chapter Five

HOW DOES ACTUAL FLYING DEVIATE FROM THAT PLANNED?

AMC draws not only on its organic assets but also on commercial augmentation to meet the peacetime airlift requirements both of the military services and of the U.S. government. A high level of peacetime demand relative to overall capacity could stress U.S. airlift assets, both organic and commercial, to the point at which they are not adequately maintained to be ready for war. On the other hand, a low level of peacetime demand relative to capacity might lead to insufficient flying hours for both (1) meeting military pilots' aging and proficiency requirements, which are necessary to ensure readiness, and (2) providing enough business to commercial carriers to induce them to be CRAF participants. At any level of demand, AMC's objective is to acquire and manage its organic assets efficiently and to purchase the right amount and types of commercial augmentation.

In this chapter, we examine the deviation of actual flying hours from those planned. The larger the deviation, the more difficult and expensive it is for AMC to adjust its flight schedules and to meet its pilots' flying requirements. Adjustments include flying organic assets with lighter payloads and canceling buys that are incentives for commercial air carriers to participate in CRAF. We will introduce two categories of deviation. First, we assess annual programmed versus actual flying hours. We then assess three metrics of planned versus actual flying hours on a monthly basis.

PROGRAMMED VERSUS ACTUAL ANNUAL FLYING HOURS

Each year, AMC prepares a Flying-Hour Program for organic assets using as its basis its pilots' aging and proficiency requirements. Then, when AMC plans the commercial augmentation that will be used, it subtracts Flying-Hour Program hours from the projected flying demand of AMC customers. The resulting excess demand is then met by commercial air carriers. The timeline in establishing the Flying-Hour Program follows that of the federal government's budget cycle. AMC submits its Flying-Hour Program to Congress for funding. After congressional appropriation, these flying hours, now in the "Congress Program,"[1] remain unchanged throughout the fiscal year. Thus, by comparing flying hours in the Congress Program with actual flying hours, we can see the deviation from programmed flying hours.[2] In Figure 5.1,[3] we plot programmed and actual flying hours reported in the annual *Command Data Books*.[4] We include additional data points from selected AMC flying-hour execution reports that were provided to us by AMC.

From 1986 to 1997, the actual annual flying hours of the C-5 exceeded the corresponding programmed hours, implying that C-5 pilots had flown more than enough to meet their aging and proficiency requirements. During FY 2000, however, the situation was reversed, with actual flying hours falling below programmed hours. Consequently, as indicated earlier in Table 2.3, C-5 CPs did not have enough flying hours to meet the aging requirements reflected in the Flying-Hour Program. For C-141s, the same phenomenon of insufficient flying hours began to appear by 1992. C-17s have been flying below programmed hours ever since their introduction into the force. The actual flying hours of

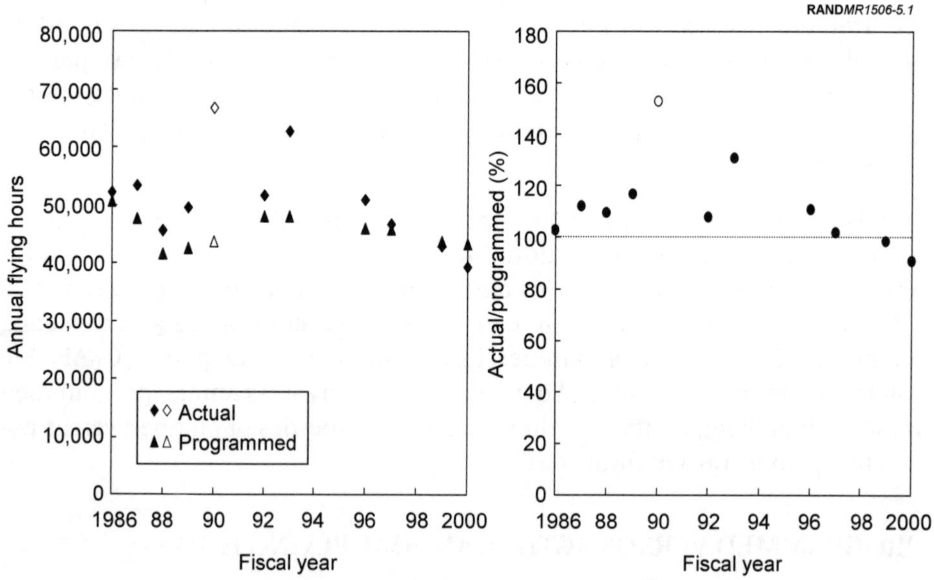

Figure 5.1—C-5 Annual Flying Hours

---

[1]The data are reported in AMC's Flying-Hour Execution Reports.

[2] In the *Command Data Books*, the Congress Program is simply listed as "the Program."

[3]See Figures A.31 to A.35 in the appendix for the C-141, C-17, C-130, KC-135, and KC-10.

[4]Unfortunately, such numbers were not reported in the *Command Data Books* for the years 1981–1985 and 1994–1998.

C-130s dropped below planned flying hours in 1999 and 2000. Therefore, all four airlifters faced insufficient flying hours at various times. In contrast, the KC-135 and KC-10 tankers have largely flown more than programmed since 1993.

These results are consistent with the flying-hour shortage found in Chapter Two but shed more light on the situation. First, when the total actual flying hours were below those programmed, there was a shortage of flying hours for CPs. This implies that the flying hours of ACs were adjusted sufficiently downward to spare enough flying hours for CPs to meet their aging requirement. Second, the programmed flying hours were estimated with little safety margin. Thus, whenever actual hours fell below programmed hours, a shortage occurred. Third, even when actual flying hours somewhat exceeded programmed hours during FY 2000, the CPs of the KC-135 and KC-10 tankers still flew fewer hours than their aging requirements called for.[5] Thus, either the CP flying hours had been programmed too low in the first place or some of the programmed CP flying hours were flown by ACs instead.

PLANNED VERSUS ACTUAL ANNUAL FLYING HOURS

In the section above, we discussed programmed annual flying hours that were generally approved by Congress before or shortly after the beginning of the fiscal year in October. As the fiscal year proceeds, AMC adjusts its flying-hour plan. The adjusted hours for organic flying appear under the heading "current program" in AMC's monthly and quarterly flying-hour execution reports. While adjustments can be made as frequently as necessary, they typically follow the schedule below.

The first adjustment is made in January, after review of the actual flying data for the first quarter of the fiscal year. At this time, AMC examines whether pilots of each aircraft type are flying enough hours to meet their aging and proficiency requirements. This generally correlates closely with which aircraft are flying more or less than programmed. If pilots of a certain type are flying less than the amount programmed during the first quarter, AMC allocates more flying hours to those pilots and their aircraft for the remainder of the fiscal year. If the overall airlift demand suddenly declines, however, the shortage can be across the board for pilots of all aircraft types—at which point AMC reduces commercial expansion buys to keep up organic flying hours. On the other hand, if it becomes apparent that the demand for certain missions will be higher than initially projected and if commercial air carriers are unsuitable for these missions,

---

[5]As shown in Table 2.3, KC-135 and KC-10 CPs flew below their aging requirements during FY 2000 and FY 2001.

AMC makes upward modifications for organic flying in the current program. In order to avoid overstressing the aircraft and pilots flying those extra missions, AMC is likely to increase commercial augmentation in the mission areas to which organic assets are diverted. The second adjustment is generally made three months later, in April and onward. In this manner, the current program is typically revised once every few months.

In the results that follow, we compare actual monthly flying hours with those in the most recent revision of the current program (which we refer to as "planned hours"). It can thus be seen that these planned numbers are not the programmed numbers at the beginning of the fiscal year; rather, they are the numbers revised throughout the year in an attempt to better match actual flying hours for the remaining months of the fiscal year. The extent to which these numbers still do not match is the discrepancy between actual and planned flying hours for a "few-month" horizon. If we compare planned and actual flying hours, we are thus measuring short-term deviations. Large deviations represent difficulties that have been encountered in predicting actual flying hours throughout the fiscal year, for which AMC might have incurred extra expenses in assembling the aircrew and aircraft at the last minute. A key cause of large deviations stems from unexpected and sudden changes in demand over a few-month horizon. For the rest of this chapter, we will examine how the deviation evolved in the 1980s and 1990s.

Figure 5.2 shows the actual and planned annual flying hours for the C-5. Other than the Gulf War years (FY 1990 and FY 1991) and the exceptional year of FY 1994,[6] AMC generally managed to match planned and actual flying hours rather well, with actual hours on average slightly above those planned. These annual numbers do not, however, reveal monthly overshoots (actual exceeding planned) or undershoots throughout a given fiscal year. Such monthly deviations can cancel each other out to yield a deceptive picture of little annual deviation or adjustment difficulty.

The monthly deviation for a given aircraft type is defined as actual monthly flying hours minus planned monthly flying hours.[7] We introduce three means of measuring the deviation of actual flying from that planned. The first measure is the absolute deviation-from-planned flying, which is the annual sum of absolute monthly deviations. The larger this measure, the larger the monthly differ-

[6]See Chapter Two for an explanation of why FY 1994 is excluded in the determination of the trend line for all aircraft types.

[7]The planned hours are those with a planning horizon ranging from zero to a few months depending on when and how many times the plan is adjusted throughout the fiscal year.

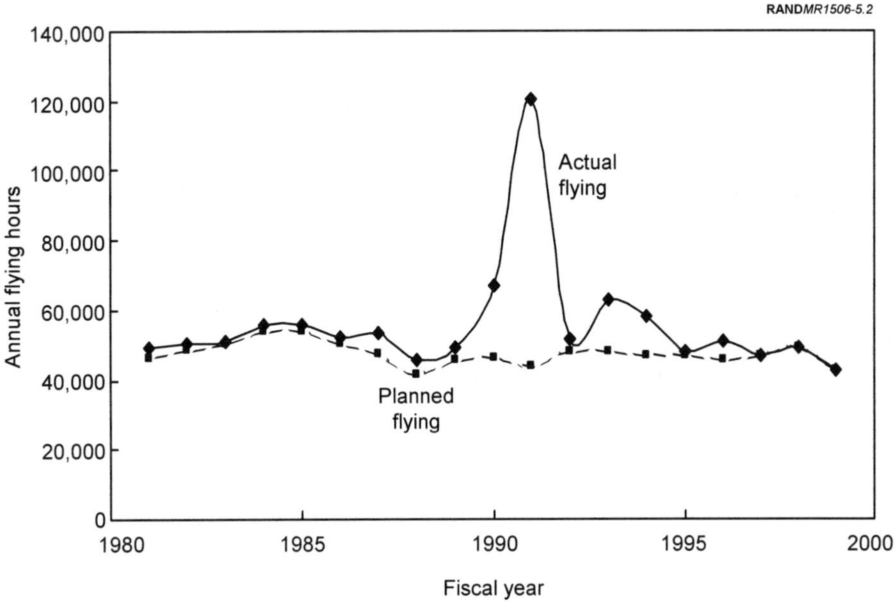

Figure 5.2—C-5 Actual Versus Planned Annual Flying Hours

ence between actual flying hours and those flying hours planned a few months before.

The second measure is peak greater-than-planned (GTP) flying, which focuses on the months in a given fiscal year in which a particular aircraft type flies more as opposed to less than planned. This measure represents the flying hours in the month with the largest GTP (the largest positive actual hours minus planned hours) flying in the year. It gauges the largest (positive) monthly deviation in the year and tells us the largest (positive) adjustment that AMC has to make.

The third measure is the length of GTP flying. This measure counts the number of consecutive months in which actual monthly flying exceeds that planned and gauges the duration in months that AMC has to sustain GTP flying. Together, these three measures provide a picture of how actual flying deviates from what was planned only a few months before.

Deviation-from-Planned Flying

Before we show the three measures outlined above, we present in Figure 5.3 a histogram of the monthly deviation (actual flying hours minus planned flying hours for a particular month) of the C-5. The difficulty one encounters in de-

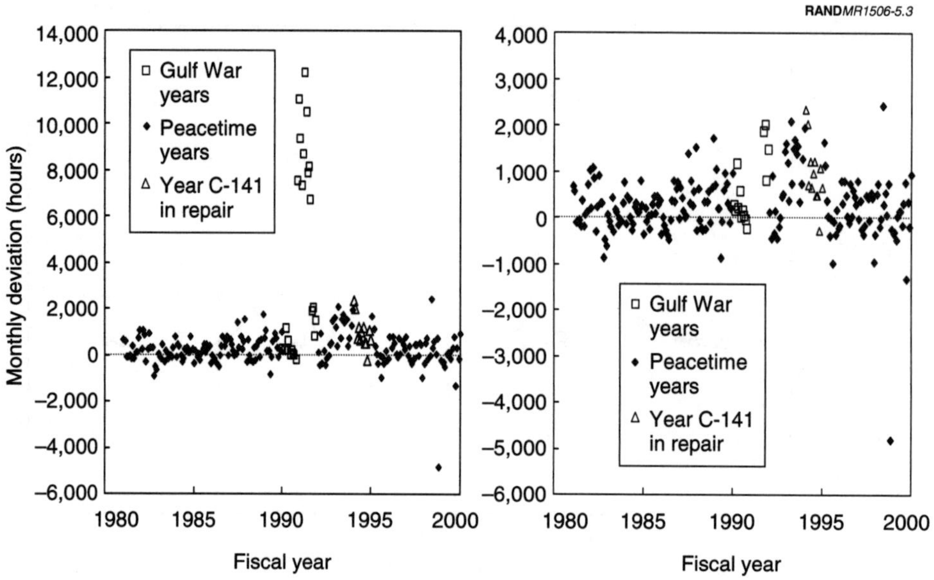

Figure 5.3—C-5 Monthly Deviation (actual minus planned flying hours)

tecting the characteristics and trend of these deviations illustrates why we need better measures. The right panel in this figure, as well as in Figures 5.4, A.36, and A.38 to A.42, is an enlargement of the left panel.

The absolute deviation-from-planned flying for the C-5 is shown in Figure 5.4. The enlarged right panel allows the trend excluding the Gulf War and the 1994 data points to be viewed more clearly. The deviation increased by 5.9 percent a year, or from around 50 flying hours per year per C-5 in the early 1980s to more than 100 hours by the late 1990s. The number of annual flying hours per C-5 in the late 1990s stood at around 750,[8] and a deviation of 100 hours translates into 13 percent of actual flying hours. The deviation was less in the 1980s because during the Cold War era, peacetime demand was governed to a greater extent by routine missions and thus remained stable. In the 1990s, by contrast, engagements unpredictably ebbed and flowed. Airlift planning thus became more difficult, and correspondingly large and frequent deviations were demonstrated. More frequent upward and downward monthly adjustments can be more costly, as flights have to be added or canceled at the last minute. Moreover, the fluctuations around the trend line in 1993 and 1998 (even when the Gulf War and the 1994 data points were excluded) were much larger than those during the 1980s.

---

[8]See Figure 2.6.

RANDMR1506-5.4

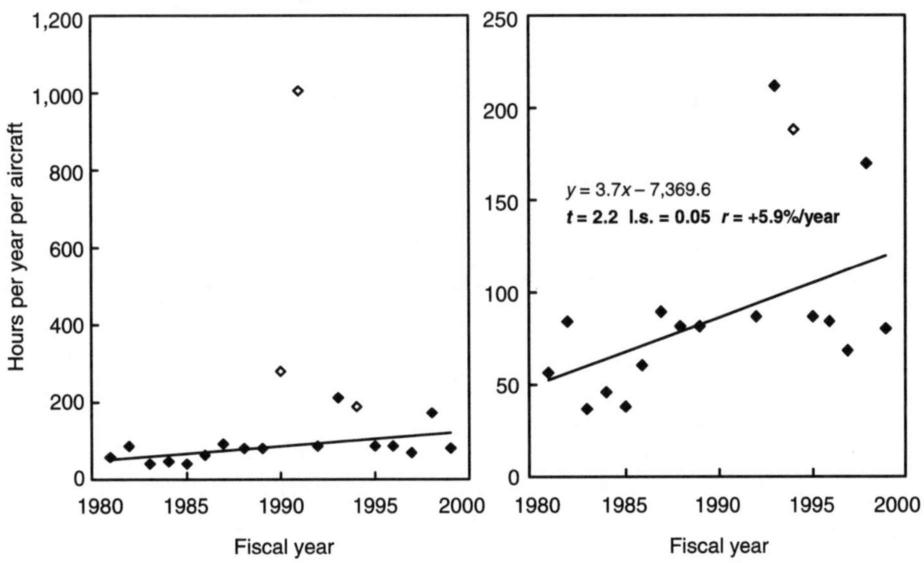

NOTE: Data points for 1990, 1991, and 1994 were excluded from the determination of the trend line.

Figure 5.4—C-5 Flying-Hour Deviation from Planned (the annual sum of absolute differences between monthly actual and planned flying hours per aircraft)

The absolute deviation-from-planned flying for the C-141 showed much larger fluctuations in the 1990s than in the 1980s, and the average trend shows a deviation increasing by 4.4 percent per year.[9]

Although only a few data points are available since 1995 for the newly introduced C-17 airlifter, the deviation for this aircraft can still be seen to have rapidly declined to about 200 hours by the late 1990s. Because the number of annual flying hours per C-17 is around 1200 hours,[10] the deviation amounted to 17 percent—a level not much different from that of the C-5. By the late 1990s, the demand for the C-17 was as predictable as that for the C-5.

C-130 deviations show a positive trend, as do those for the C-5 and C-141. The increase in deviation, however, amounted to 8.1 percent, which was greater than comparable increases for the C-5 and C-141. We have no similar data for the KC-135 and KC-10 tankers.

---

[9]See Figures A.36 to A.38 in the appendix for the C-141, C-17, and C-130.

[10]See Figure A.7 in the appendix.

In sum, the deviations of actual from planned flying hours increased for the C-5, C-141, and C-130 over the past two decades. The deviation for the C-17 was significant when the aircraft was first introduced, but by 1997 that deviation had declined to a level similar to that of the C-5.

Peak Greater-than-Planned Flying

Among the positive monthly deviations of actual flying hours from those planned in a given year, how large is the largest deviation? The peak monthly deviation shows the largest monthly positive miss in AMC's flying-hour plan during a given year. Table 5.1 shows the peak GTP flying levels for the C-5, C-141, C-17, and C-130.[11] The peak GTP for the C-5 trended upward at a rate of 4.3 percent per year. In the early 1980s, the peak GTP was about 10 hours per month per C-5, or roughly 17 percent of the actual 60 hours of flying.[12] The trend line indicates that the peak GTP doubled from the 1980s on to reach a level of about 20 hours per month per C-5 by the late 1990s. The greater the peak GTP, the more difficult and costly it is likely to be to reschedule flights quickly, and the more likely it is that the quality of life of the pilots who must staff these short-notice flights will be negatively affected. There were larger fluctuations in the 1990s than in the 1980s.[13]

Table 5.1 also shows the peak GTP flying levels for the C-141. The rate of change was 4.3 percent per year, and was similar to that for the C-5. Also, as with the C-5, there were more fluctuations in the 1990s than in the 1980s.[14] The newly deployed C-17 airlifter has too few data points to indicate whether the peak GTP will level off at 45 hours per month.[15] As with the C-5 and C-141, the peak GTP flying level of the C-130 showed an upward trend, but its 9.3 percent rate of increase per year was roughly twice that of the C-5 and C-141 (see Table 5.1).[16]

In sum, the peak GTP showed an upward trend for the C-5, C-141, C-17, and C-130. In other words, the largest positive monthly adjustment in flying hours

[11]See also Figures A.39 to A.42 in the appendix.

[12]The figure of 60 hours was calculated by dividing the annual number of about 700 hours during the early 1980s, as shown in Figure 2.6, by 12 months.

[13]See Figure A.39 in the appendix.

[14]See Figure A.40 in the appendix.

[15]See Figure A.41 in the appendix.

[16]See also Figure A.42 in the appendix.

Table 5.1

Peak GTP Flying Hours

Aircraft	Data Period (fiscal years)	Rate of Change (%/year)	*t*-Test Statistic	Level of Significance
C-5	1981–1999	+4.3	1.8	0.10
C-141	1981–1999	+4.3	0.9	0.41
C-17	1994–1999	+25.0	1.5	0.22
C-130	1981–1999	**+9.3**	**4.4**	**0.00**

NOTE: Data points for 1990, 1991, and 1994 were excluded from the determination of the numbers in the third to fifth columns. Bold entries indicate that the probability of a nonzero trend (rate of change) is 95 percent or higher.

during a year increased between the 1980s and the 1990s. We have no data on the peak GTP for the KC-135 and KC-10 tankers.

Length of Greater-than-Planned Flying

In the previous two subsections, we determined the yearly sum of the absolute monthly deviations from planned flying hours and the largest of the monthly GTP flying hours in a given fiscal year. This subsection looks at the length of uninterrupted monthly GTP flying hours or simply the length of GTP flying hours. In it, we measure how long a span of monthly GTP flying hours lasts. If there are four months in a row in which monthly actual flying hours exceed those planned, the length is considered to be four months. A longer length of time places an increasing burden on the air mobility system, which must sustain the effort of quickly gathering extra aircraft and personnel.

Table 5.2 shows the length of uninterrupted monthly GTP flying hours for the C-5, C-141, C-17, and C-130.[17] The C-5 shows a flat trend line, with the average GTP flying-hour period lasting about three months.[18] In other words, the duration of GTP flying was as long in the 1990s as in the 1980s. The fluctuation in duration was wide in the 1990s, just as it was in the 1980s. Thus, one cannot say that the situation was worse in the 1990s.

The length of GTP flying for the C-141, shown in Table 5.2,[19] had characteristics similar to those for the C-5—a flat trend line with wide fluctuation both in the 1980s and in the 1990s. The duration was two months as opposed to three months for the C-5. Even the C-17,[20] for which few data points were available,

---

[17]See also Figures A.43 to A.46 in the appendix.

[18]See Figure A.43 in the appendix.

[19]See also Figure A.44 in the appendix.

[20]See Figure A.45 in the appendix.

mimicked the patterns of the C-5 and C-141: The GTP duration was two months, similar to that of the C-141. Finally, the pattern for the C-130, shown in Table 5.2, showed a flat trend similar to that seen with the C-5, C-141, and C-17 and a two-month duration akin to that for the C-141 and C-17. For the C-130, there was more fluctuation in duration in the 1980s than in the 1990s.

In sum, the average duration of GTP flying hours was for two to three months—a duration that did not change substantially from the 1980s to the 1990s. The fluctuation in duration was also relatively similar in the 1980s and 1990s except in the case of the C-130, which showed a decrease in fluctuation. Overall, the air mobility system was not burdened more by the duration of GTP flying hours in the 1990s. We have no data on the length of GTP flying hours for the KC-135 and KC-10 tankers.

Table 5.2

Length of Uninterrupted Monthly GTP Flying Hours

Aircraft	Data Period (fiscal years)	Rate of Change (%/year)	*t*-Test Statistic	Level of Significance
C-5	1981–1999	–0.3	0.1	0.90
C-141	1981–1999	–0.1	0.0	0.98
C-17	1994–1999	+3.3	0.5	0.63
C-130	1981–1999	–1.1	0.6	0.56

NOTE: Data points for 1990, 1991, and 1994 were excluded from the determination of the numbers in the third to fifth columns.

Chapter Six

IS COMMERCIAL AUGMENTATION TAKING A LARGER SHARE OF FLYING HOURS?

As previously discussed, there are two sources of funds to support AMC pilots' flying-hour requirements. The preferred source is TWCF. When AMC undertakes airlift missions for its customers such as the Army and the Air Force, its flying expenses are reimbursed by customers through TWCF. On the other hand, if AMC asks a commercial air carrier to perform the requested airlift service, most if not all of the fee paid by the customer goes to the commercial carrier, not to AMC. The other source of funding is derived from the Air Force's allocation of its O&M fund to AMC. The AMC O&M fund not only supports operations at the headquarters and air bases but also pays for the flying hours necessary for aging and proficiency that are not reimbursed by customers. These flying hours can be for TTF or for JA/ATT—functions that are not performed during service missions for customers and are thus not reimbursed. Moreover, when AMC is short of pilot-training flying hours, it may fly missions without any customer cargo in order to generate flying hours. In such cases, the missions will not be reimbursed by customers, and the expenses will have to come from the O&M fund.

O&M and TWCF funds account for the bulk of AMC's annual operating budget. In FY 1999, for example, these funds amounted to 91 percent of that budget.[1] We therefore focus on these two sources of funds (see Figure 6.1). O&M and TWCF combined increased by 15 percent between 1984 and 1999 (see the left panel of Figure 6.1). However, the reimbursable component (the TWCF share of total funds) declined 1.8 percent per year over the past two decades (see the right panel of Figure 6.1). In 1984, TWCF accounted for 70 percent of total funds, but by 1999 this figure had declined to 51 percent. In other words, AMC's internal funds supported only 30 percent of its expenses in 1984, whereas by 1999 such funds supported 49 percent of those expenses. Because

[1]The remaining 9 percent included items such as the defense health program and military family housing. See *Command Data Book*, November 1999, p. 63.

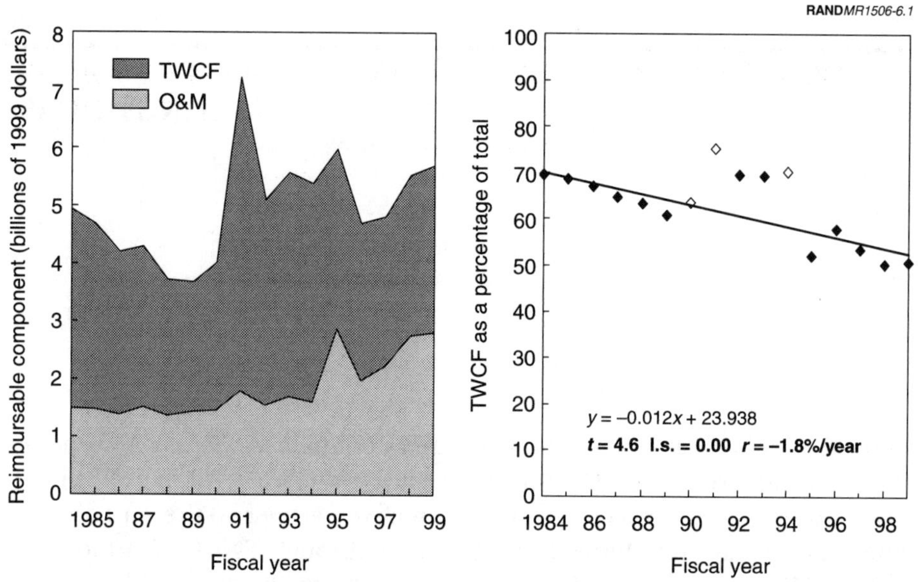

NOTE: Data points for 1990, 1991, and 1994 were excluded from the determination of the trend line.

Figure 6.1—The Reimbursable Component of the Operating Budget Declined

AMC's sole mission is to provide airlift to military and other government customers during both peacetime and war, one can argue that AMC should have its operating expenses reimbursed by its customers to the maximum extent possible. The decreasing share of expenses paid by customers, as reflected in the smaller TWCF share, is of concern.

AMC customers can bypass TWCF to obtain certain airlift services. In FY 1999, AMC and the General Services Administration (GSA) signed a Worldwide Express (WWX) contract for the international air delivery of small packages weighing up to 150 pounds. The intention was to remove small-package shipments from AMC's ports, as commercial carriers could handle such shipments at a lower cost. Small-package shipments, however, account for roughly 40 percent of all pieces shipped while representing only 5 pecent to 10 percent of the weight moving through AMC's ports, and TWCF now loses this revenue. WWX supplements the already-existing GSA Express Small Package Program for the domestic air delivery of packages weighing up to 150 pounds to destinations more than 500 miles away. Tenders are also offered by CRAF carriers to provide transportation services; these are negotiated directly with AMC customers. Tenders are used for shipments exceeding 150 pounds to prevent competition with WWX.

Although AMC standardizes and approves a carrier's tender prior to its use, the organization does not oversee these negotiations. Because tenders are not part of TWCF, however, they further decrease the share of TWCF for AMC. Direct Vendor Delivery (DVD) and Premium Service are two more types of contracts that lie outside TWCF. DVD is a commercial acquisition contract that involves the manufacture and delivery of products. Premium Service is a storage and transportation arrangement in which materiel is typically stored in a commercial storage depot that is collocated with a worldwide air parcel carrier hub such as that of FedEx.[2] These contracts will continue to lower the revenues that could have gone to TWCF for AMC to share.

Airlift services provided by commercial air carriers to help meet AMC customers' demand, procured through TWCF, represent commercial augmentation (and their funding is derived from commercial TWCF). Even in the post–Cold War era, there have been many peacetime contingencies that have provided business and incentives to CRAF members (see Table 6.1). AMC uses funds from three components to meet its customers' airlift demand: military O&M, military TWCF, and commercial TWCF. During peacetime, the first two components fluctuated more than the third.[3]

As of FY 1999, commercial augmentation accounted for $900,000 of the $2.9 billion TWCF, and organic airlift expenses accounted for the remaining $2.0 billion. O&M expenses stood at $2.8 billion. Over the years, the TWCF share of the overall budget (TWCF and O&M combined) not only has diminished (as shown in Figure 6.1) but has been increasingly captured by the commercial air carriers, leaving even less for AMC. Figure 6.2 shows an increasing share of the TWCF going to commercial providers (23 percent in 1981 as compared to 32 percent in 1999). When more funds are allocated to commercial augmentation, fewer are available to support AMC peacetime operations. This is troubling when AMC does not have enough flying hours for its own pilots.[4]

AMC prefers channel cargo missions for pilot training because they are both stable and sizable and can be planned well in advance. However, the commercial carriers have captured an increasing share of these missions over the past

---

[2]Ken Reynolds, RAND, internal trip notes, April 17–19, 2000.

[3]See Figure A.47 in the appendix.

[4]If there were fewer TWCF funds to support the flying-hour requirement, AMC would have to rely more on the O&M fund. To us, these two sources of funds are very different, because we believe that AMC customers should pay for AMC operations as much as possible, with Air Force subsidies used as a last resort.

Table 6.1

Participation of Commercial Air Carriers in Peacetime Contingencies

Location	Operation	Year Operation Began	Cargo Delivered (tons)	Passengers Delivered
Philippines	Fiery Vigil	1991	2,412	16,882
Northern Iraq	Provide Comfort[a]	1991	2,898	18,294
Former Soviet Union	Provide Hope	1992	4,895	100
Bosnia	Provide Promise	1992	145	2,345
Somalia	Restore Hope	1992	463	52,136
Rwanda	Support Hope	1994	2,138	548
Cuba	Sea Signal V	1994	848	29,524
Panama	Panama Haven/Safe Haven	1994	NA	4,647
Haiti	Phoenix Shark	1994	1,823	33,546
Cuba	Safe Haven/Safe Passage	1994	0	4,050
Persian Gulf	Vigilant Warrior	1994	1,389	12,010
Bosnia	Joint Endeavor[b]	1995	7,300	41,000

SOURCE: Congressional Budget Office, *Moving U.S. Forces: Options for Strategic Mobility,* February 1997, p. 85.

[a]As of August 1995.

[b]As of January 1997.

two decades, with that share rising from 24 percent in 1981 to 46 percent in 1999, or 5 percent per year.[5]

In Figure 6.3, the commercial share of the TWCF fund (shown in Figure 6.2 as the reimbursable fund) is broken down into mission categories.[6] By 1999, airlifting cargo for channel missions, AMC's favorite mission, accounted for $330 million and represented the largest fraction of the fund allocated to commercial augmentation. The next two categories, "other passengers" and "channel passengers," together represent the expenses for transporting passengers and accounted for $400 million, even higher than the amount spent for channel cargo. Without a dedicated passenger-carrying aircraft fleet, AMC

[5]Data on commercial channel cargo and mail are segregated, while they are aggregated under "channel cargo" for military airlifters. We have therefore added "mail" to "commercial channel cargo" in Figures A.48 and A.50. Had "mail" not been added, the increase per year would have been even higher, at 9 percent as opposed to 5 percent shown in Figure A.48.

[6]During the Gulf War, AMC greatly increased commercial augmentation in two categories: other passengers and channel cargo. Because AMC does not have airlifters dedicated to passenger carrying, it had to contract commercial carriers for delivering soldiers to the theater. The destinations at the theater are not necessarily the channel APODs, and thus the volume for the category of "other than channel passengers" surged. At the same time, the demand for both channel cargo and theater cargo delivery increased during this period. AMC thus had to divert aircraft that had previously been delivering channel cargo to deliver cargo into the theater. It contracted commercial carriers to fill the gap and meet the heightened demand for channel cargo missions.

RANDMR1506-6.2

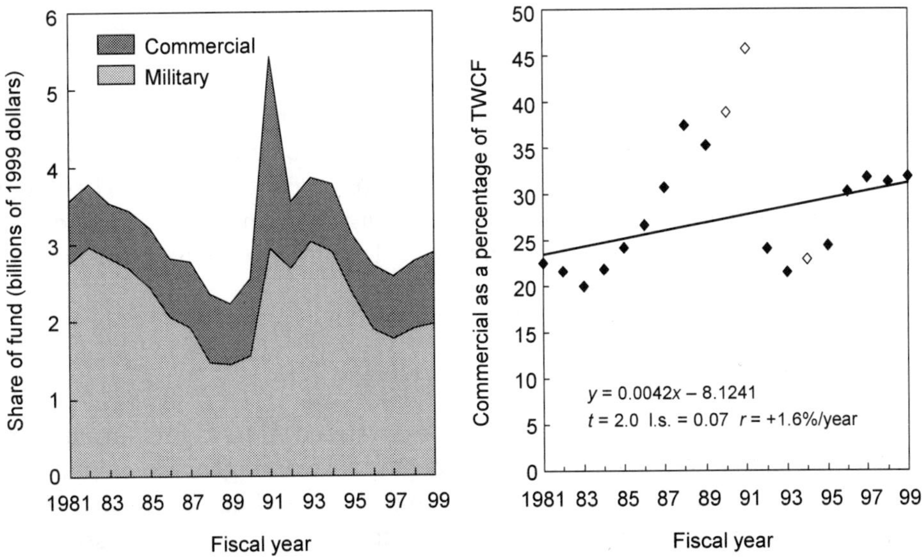

NOTE: Data points for 1990, 1991, and 1994 were excluded from the determination of the trend line.

Figure 6.2—Commercial Carriers Accounted for an Increasing Share of the Reimbursable Fund

RANDMR1506-6.3

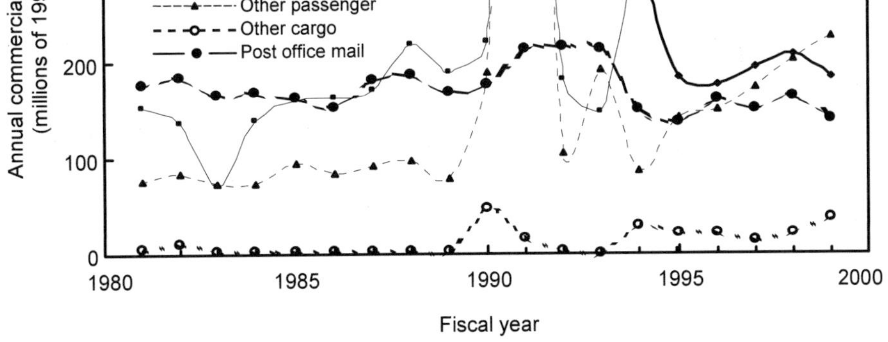

NOTE: Both channel cargo and other passenger rose to about $900 million each in FY 1991.

Figure 6.3—Annual Commercial Augmentation

cannot take back much of this business. Thus, an option currently available to AMC for retaining more flying hours for its own pilots is to keep more cargo as opposed to passenger missions in house.

In channel passenger miles,[7] the commercial air carriers continued to dominate this business at 90 percent.[8] For channel cargo in ton-miles, the commercial providers captured an increasing share: from 16 percent in 1981 to 41 percent in 1999, or 7 percent a year.[9] Thus, AMC has long been unable to compete with commercial air carriers for passengers and is losing cargo delivery business to the private sector.

FREE TRAVEL SUBSIDY

When there are empty seats in organic or chartered AMC flights for channel missions, military personnel and civilian personnel working for the military can travel free, as can their dependents. Although this trend had been decreasing, 65 percent of the passengers on AMC organic flights, or 132,000 passengers, were still nonpaying customers in 1999 (see the "military free" line in Figure 6.4).[10] On the other hand, the share of nonpaying passengers in AMC-chartered commercial channel flights showed an upward trend, increasing from 11 percent in 1989 to 29 percent, or 110,000 nonpaying passengers, by 1999. In essence, then, AMC is paying for the services' fringe benefit of free travel. If the services were made to pay for their share, AMC would be reimbursed for this travel.

---

[7]In data provided to the *Command Data Book*, AMC uses miles for paying passengers only. Miles for nonpaying passengers are not included.

[8]See Figure A.49 in the appendix.

[9]See Figure A.50 in the appendix. The increases measured in ton-miles are higher than those measured in dollars, as shown in Figure A.48 in the appendix. This implies that the dollar-per-ton-mile rate charged by AMC became less competitive with that of commercial carriers during 1981–1999.

[10]We focus here on passengers carried during channel missions. While AMC organic assets and commercial air carriers also carry passengers during other missions such as SAAMs, those passengers are not included. In FY 1999, AMC carried 70,500 paying passengers and 132,000 nonpaying passengers on C-141s, C-5s, C-130s, KC-10s, KC-135s, and C-17s during channel missions. In the same year, AMC also contracted commercial chartered flights to carry 257,000 paying and 107,000 nonpaying passengers during channel missions. Thus, the commercial percentage in terms of number of paying passengers was 78 percent in FY 1999, while that in terms of passenger miles was a comparable 86 percent (see Figure A.49 in the appendix). Moreover, based on these channel numbers here and in Figure A.49, we calculated that DoD paying passengers averaged 3800 miles per trip in FY 1999.

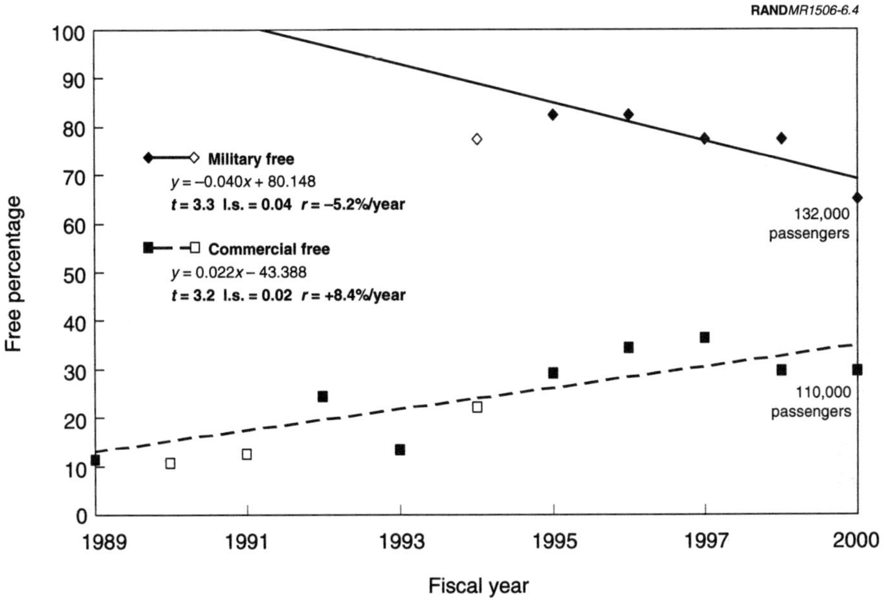

NOTE: Data points for 1990, 1991, and 1994 were excluded from the determination of the trend lines.

Figure 6.4—Percentage of Nonpaying Channel Passengers

Chapter Seven

POTENTIAL PROBLEMS IN ACHIEVING COST-EFFECTIVE OPERATIONS

In this chapter, we summarize the potential problems (identified in Chapters Two to Six) that could negatively affect AMC's ability to meet peacetime airlift demand and maintain wartime readiness, together with some incentives for CRAF participation.

FLYING-HOUR SHORTAGES IN FY 2000 AND FY 2001 AND THEIR LIKELY RECURRENCE

Before the beginning of a fiscal year, AMC submits a Flying-Hour Program to Congress for appropriation. These programmed flying hours reflect the number of hours needed during the coming fiscal year to meet AMC pilots' aging and proficiency requirements. During FY 1999 and FY 2000, all airlifters (the C-5, C-141, C-17, and C-130) flew fewer hours than programmed, while the tankers (the KC-135 and KC-10) still managed to fly more hours than programmed.[1] However, the CPs of all airlifters and tankers failed to meet their aging requirement during FY 2000 and FY 2001.[2] ACs also flew considerably less during this period. ACs, however, were able to meet their proficiency requirements because they have fewer required flying hours than do CPs.

In the future, the flying-hour shortage during peacetime may worsen from time to time for two reasons. First, in the post–Cold War era, one cannot predict the frequency or level of peacetime military intervention or how long such intervention will last. Overall peacetime demand can be low for a long stretch of time. Second, while peacetime demand can fluctuate widely from year to year, wartime mobility requirements have been on an upward trend.

---

[1]See Figure 5.1 and Figures A.31 to A.35 in the appendix.

[2]See Figure 2.7, Table 2.3, and Figures A.11 to A.15 in the appendix.

The latest official planning document calls for higher wartime mobility requirements of 54.5 MTM/D.[3] In the aftermath of September 11, however, General John Handy, Commander in Chief of the U.S. Transportation Command (USTRANSCOM), said that the new airlift requirement will undoubtedly be higher than 54.5 MTM/D in light of increased lift needs for a "world war on terrorism." General Handy added that the requirement would have to factor in increased demands for homeland defense as well.[4] It is unclear at this time how much of the new airlift demand will be needed in peacetime as opposed to wartime. If the increased wartime burden continues to be shared by military and commercial air carriers in their current proportions, more military pilots will be needed, and more flying hours will be necessary to keep those trained and proficient in flying during peacetime. The Air Force has already agreed to buy 60 more C-17s for a total of 180 and will probably seek another 42 or more.[5] Moreover, since September 11, commercial air carriers have been reducing their capacity in efforts to cope with a sharp drop in air travel that may well last indefinitely. This reduction can lead to a corresponding cut in carriers' wartime commitment to CRAF. To compensate, AMC may have to further increase the number of its aircraft and pilots. This increased number of pilots would require still more flying hours for training.

The need to meet flying-hour requirements should be considered in all proposed Air Force programs, and compensatory adjustments should be made either within these new programs or in other programs. For example, the Air Force has proposed a highly unusual offer to entice private air cargo firms to buy the BC-17, a commercial-variant of the C-17.[6] The Air Force proposed that BC-17 buyers be guaranteed some 20 percent of the peacetime annual airlift business that AMC contracts to commercial air carriers. This guarantee could further decrease peacetime flying hours for military pilots because a portion of peacetime business might be taken away from existing CRAF participants, for whom such business is a major incentive to join CRAF.

---

[3]The latest revision of requirement MRS-05 calls for a minimum of 51.1 MTM/D. This is only slightly higher than the 49.7 MTM/D determined during the 1995 MRS-BURU. The missions and variations in assumptions examined in MRS-05, however, generated a range of airlift demands extending up to 67 MTM/D. The chairman of the Joint Chiefs of Staff, the service chiefs, and the commanders in chief (CINCs) "support the establishment of a requirement of 54.5 MTM[/D] of airlift capability as the minimum moderate risk capability to support the national military strategy." See the footnote on the CRAF program and MRS-05 in Chapter Two.

[4]See "Handy: Sept. 11, QDR Likely to Lead to an Increase in Lift Requirement," *Inside the Air Force*, October 12, 2001.

[5]See "Despite Heavy Demands, AMC Predicts No Change in Airlift Requirement," *Inside the Air Force*, March 8, 2002.

[6]See Peter Pae, "Boeing Renews Push for Commercial C-17 Variant," *Los Angeles Times*, January 31, 2001.

On the other hand, small-scale contingencies similar to those in Bosnia and Kosovo as well as new counterterrorism contingencies during peacetime might place a high demand on AMC organic assets from time to time. AMC should thus develop the flexibility to meet fluctuating demand, both high and low.

THE ACTUAL NUMBER OF COPILOTS AND AIRCRAFT COMMANDERS EXCEEDED THAT AUTHORIZED

Since 1986, the actual total number of full-time CPs and ACs at AMC has exceeded the number authorized in a trend that has continued upward. During FY 2001, however, this number decreased from about 10 percent over authorization during FY 1998–2000 to only 4 percent over the authorized number.[7]

Over the past two decades, the actual numbers of CPs and ACs increased. During FY 2001, however, these numbers were only 3 percent to 5 percent above what Congress had authorized.

THE ACTUAL COPILOT-TO-AIRCRAFT COMMANDER RATIO DEVIATED FROM THAT AUTHORIZED

During FY 2001, the actual CP/AC ratios for airlifters (the C-5, C-141, C-17, and C-130) exceeded those authorized by Congress. Conversely, tankers (the KC-10 and KC-135) have had too many ACs relative to CPs in recent years if the mix is based on what Congress authorized.[8]

LESS PILOTING DURING TRAINING

The current AMC rule for meeting aging and proficiency requirements credits aircraft flying hours to every member of the aircrew regardless of whether an individual is piloting an aircraft from a pilot seat or is merely observing from somewhere else in that aircraft. Thus, an increase in the average number of pilots per flight indicates that pilots are getting less piloting opportunity and experience.

The airlifters (the C-5, C-141, C-17, and C-130) all exhibited a trend characterized by an increasing number of pilots per flight.[9] The average number of pilots per C-5 flight, for example, increased at a rate of 2 percent per year. Although C-141s will be retired in a few years, its uptrend of 3.2 percent per year will still

---

[7]See Figure 3.1.

[8]See Figures A.29 and A.30 in the appendix.

[9]See Figures 4.1 to 4.4. On the other hand, we had no corresponding data for the tankers.

be a concern if reduced piloting affects the quality of training. The C-17 showed a large uptrend of 9.6 percent per year, but the trend for this newly deployed aircraft can still flatten so as to become more favorable as its operations mature. The C-130 trend is not a major concern because its uptrend was only 0.6 percent per year.

INCREASING DEVIATION FROM FLYING PLAN

The actual flying hours of the C-5, C-141, and C-130 showed increasing deviation[10] from planned hours even though the flying plan is adjusted every few months throughout the fiscal year.[11] By the late 1990s, this deviation was roughly that of the early 1980s. Scrambling to meet surprise demand makes the scheduling of flights and maintenance more difficult and costly while also reducing pilots' quality of life.

In any given year, actual flying hours in some months exceed what was planned only a few months before. The month in which the excess is greatest is that with the peak GTP flying. The C-5, C-141, and C-130 showed increasing levels of peak GTP flying.[12] If this trend continues, AMC will have to assemble a larger number of aircraft and personnel in a hurry to meet the largest monthly deviation in flying hours. Again, the doubling or more of peak GTP flying from the early 1980s to the late 1990s could negatively affect scheduling and quality of life.

In contrast, the duration of uninterrupted monthly GTP flying for the four airlifters—the C-5, C-141, C-17, and C-130—showed little change over the past two decades.[13] Thus, when actual flying in a given month exceeded the amount in a frequently updated plan, the excess lasted for roughly the same number of months in the 1990s as it did in the 1980s. As a result, one cannot say that GTP flying persists longer now than before.

---

[10]The deviation is the sum of absolute monthly deviations in a given fiscal year.

[11]See Figure 5.4 and Figures A.36 and A.38 in the appendix. On the other hand, we did not have tanker data for deviations discussed in this section.

[12]See Figures A.39, A.40, and A.42 in the appendix. The recently deployed C-17s also showed increasing peak GTP flying. However, there are not enough data to indicate the trend for matured C-17s.

[13]See Figures A.43 to A.46 in the appendix.

ENGAGEMENT MISSIONS ACCOUNTED FOR A GROWING SHARE OF MISSIONS

For all four airlifters (the C-5, C-141, C-17, and C-130), engagement missions accounted for a growing share of flying hours in the 1990s.[14] Many of these missions are for short-notice peacetime contingencies, which are more difficult and costly to schedule and more disruptive to the lives of personnel. For the C-5, these missions accounted for only 11 percent of all missions flown in 1981 but represented 68 percent of those missions by 1999. For the C-141, the share increased from 26 percent in 1981 to 38 percent in 1999. The share for the recently deployed C-17 increased from 9 percent in 1995 to 46 percent by 1999 but could stabilize quickly. The share for the C-130 increased from 21 percent in 1981 to 40 percent in 1999.

Both AMC and its pilots favor channel missions because such missions cover many training elements and can be planned well in advance. For the C-5, C-141, and C-130, however, the share of these missions declined as a percentage of total missions flown. For the C-5, the share declined sharply from 68 percent in 1981 to 15 percent by 1999; for the C-141, from 54 percent to 29 percent; and for the C-130, from 19 percent to 7 percent.

FEWER OF AMC'S FLYING EXPENSES WERE BEING REIMBURSED BY CUSTOMERS

The TWCF share of AMC's operating budget declined during the period studied from 70 percent in 1984 to 51 percent by 1999.[15] AMC was less able to recoup its training and operating expenses from the reimbursable account. This is not desirable because the government has to subsidize more for AMC operations. Worse, commercial air carriers took an increasing proportion of the TWCF fund, leaving even less money with which to reimburse AMC's flying expenses.[16] The commercial share increased from 23 percent in 1981 to 32 percent in 1999. Commercial penetration has been particularly prominent in channel cargo, which is AMC's favorite mission category for pilot training, and in mail, which together rose at a rate of 5 percent per year from 24 percent in 1981 to 46 percent in revenue dollar terms.[17] In ton-mile terms, this increase was even higher at 7.1 percent per year, rising from 16 percent in 1981 to 41

---

[14]See also Figure 2.12, and Figures A.23 to A.25 in the appendix. On the other hand, we had no similar data on tankers.

[15]See Figure 6.1.

[16]See Figure 6.2.

[17]See Figure A.48 in the appendix.

percent in 1999.[18] In addition, commercial providers have continued to dominate channel passenger miles since 1981, capturing 90 percent of this business.[19] AMC has been losing market share in channel cargo and has not been able to compete in passenger transport. Allowing commercial providers to assume a greater portion of the airlifting burden is acceptable only if AMC has the flexibility to increase and decrease its commercial buy in any particular year to accommodate its flying capability and requirement.

We also found that the percentages of channel passengers riding free on both organic and AMC-chartered commercial flights were significant, standing at 65 percent and 29 percent, respectively, in FY 1999. This too represented a loss of revenue to AMC.[20]

---

[18]See Figure A.50 in the appendix.

[19]See Figure A.49 in the appendix.

[20]See Figure 6.4.

Chapter Eight

SUGGESTED CORRECTIVE MEASURES FOR IDENTIFIED PROBLEMS

In previous chapters, we identified potential problems AMC faces in managing its peacetime air mobility operations. These problems can also affect wartime operations by hindering AMC's readiness and by discouraging its commercial partners from participating in CRAF. In this chapter, we suggest corrective measures to alleviate the problems that have previously been identified. We first address AMC's recurring flying-hour shortage and loss of revenue. We then deal with other problems.

DEALING WITH THE RECURRING FLYING-HOUR SHORTAGE AND REVENUE LOSS

The most serious problem thus far identified is that AMC pilots will from time to time have insufficient flying hours with which to meet their aging and proficiency requirements. Thus, we first suggest measures that can address this issue when it recurs. These measures should be flexible and even reversible because peacetime demand can also be high and may overstress AMC's ability both to meet such demand and to maintain wartime readiness. We will therefore expand our discussion on how AMC can use airlift capability in the commercial sector to smooth the intensity of its peacetime operations by contracting out more flying hours when overall airlift demand from the military is high and by withholding more when demand is low.

We will discuss measures to eliminate the recurring flying-hour shortage before we describe those intended to resolve the often-associated problem of loss of revenue. This is because once flying hours become sufficient, other problems—including loss of revenue—become easier to resolve. First, however, we must review the measures AMC has implemented to correct the flying-hour shortage.

Offer Measures Beyond Those Taken by AMC

AMC has taken a number of steps to deal with insufficient flying hours. First, AMC cut $89 million[1] from its international cargo buy for FY 2001, thereby reducing the flying hours diverted to commercial air carriers (see Figure 8.1). However, this action was insufficient to eliminate the shortfall during FY 2001.

Second, to alleviate the flying-hour shortage for C-130 CPs, AMC has been considering the possibility of reducing the aging requirement from 29 hours to 24 or 25 hours per month and the total hours required for promotion to AC from 1000 hours to 900 hours. However, AMC needs to show that this requirement can be reduced without affecting training.

Third, AMC decided not to correct the flying-hour shortage for C-141 CPs, because C-141s are being retired. There is, however, a problem associated with

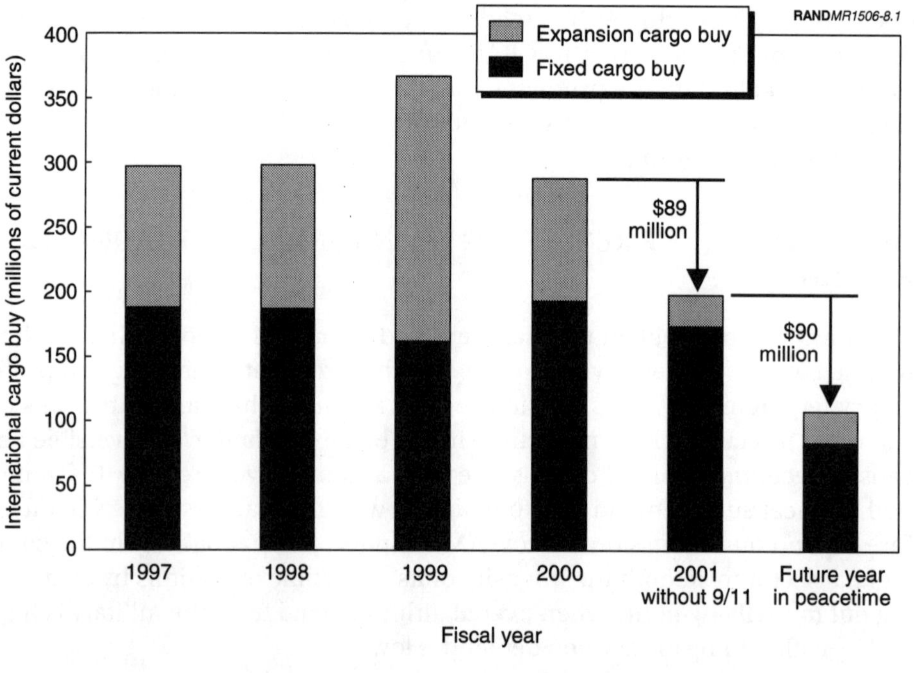

Figure 8.1—AMC Can Reduce Its International Cargo Buy to Generate More Organic Flying

---

[1]The actual reduction during FY 2001 was $77 million. In September 2001, however, the cargo buy was $12 million above normal because of post–September 11 activities. Thus, the cut would have been $89 million without those activities. We are interested in the adequacy of flying hours for pilot training during peacetime operations. In other words, without relying on contingencies such as OEF, how much cargo buy would have to be cut in order to retain sufficient flying hours for organic pilots?

this approach. Because C-141 pilots will be transferred to fly other aircraft such as C-17s their earned flying hours will count toward their requirement for promotion regardless of the aircraft to which they are assigned. Thus, reducing CP flying will delay CPs' promotion to AC. In any case, AMC needs to show that reducing flying hours will still allow for adequate training and will not affect flight safety both in the C-141 and, later, in other aircraft types.

Fourth, AMC has planned to eliminate insufficient flying hours for CPs of C-5s and C-17s by flying channel cargo missions more frequently and with lighter payloads. We estimated, however, that the extra cost involved in sustaining this approach would be approximately $70 million a year.[2] We also suggest that less expensive methods be used to reduce the flying-hour shortage.[3] One might argue that $70 million is only about 1 percent of AMC's annual budget—a negligible amount considering that its total authority for FY 1999 was $6.2 billion. We disagree for several reasons, the first of which is that $70 million annually in absolute terms is not a small sum. In addition, the extra expense involved solves the flying-hour shortage only for C-5 and C-17 CPs and amounts to 11 percent of the flying-hour cost of C-5s and C-17s—a sum that is not insignificant. Moreover, if AMC used the approach of flying more frequently and with lighter payloads to eliminate the flying-hour shortage as a whole, it would incur an additional annual cost of $144 million for generating enough flying hours for the CPs of its other airlifters (the C-141s and C-130s) and tankers (the KC-135s and KC-10s).[4] Flying empty also projects a wasteful image, particularly if there are cheaper ways to address the shortage. Finally, in today's era, the flying-hour shortage can at times be much worse than those in FY 2000 and FY 2001. Flying more frequently and with lesser payloads is thus a costly solution.

Fifth, when the flight crew planned consists of two ACs and one CP, AMC has encouraged wing commanders to replace the second AC with a CP.[5] As shown

---

[2]As of March 31, 2001, we projected that C-17 CPs would be 8700 hours short and C-5 CPs, 3100 short for the full fiscal year of 2001 if AMC were to fly the organic aircraft as much during the second half as in the first half of the fiscal year. We multiplied these hours by the corresponding variable costs per CP flying hour to obtain the figure of $70 million. In reality, AMC was willing to incur extra expenses in flying C-17s and C-5s more frequently and with lighter loads during the second half of FY 2001, reducing C-17 CPs to 4300 hours short in flying and C-5 CPs to 1400 hours short. Eliminating the remaining shortage during FY 2001 would cost $34 million. However, the total cost to eliminate the shortage by flying more with lesser payloads would be $70 million a year at a peacetime demand level of FY 2001 (without factoring in the September 11 attacks and their aftermath).

[3]These methods will be discussed in subsequent sections.

[4]We used the same methodology as that for the C-17 and C-5. In FY 2001, the actual shortages were reduced somewhat to 2000 hours for C-141 CPs, 19,000 for C-130 CPs, 2000 for KC-135 CPs, and 4500 for KC-10 CPs. The cost to eliminate the remaining shortage by flying more would be $125 million.

[5]AMC sent a bulletin to wing commanders in October 2000 to encourage them to adopt this measure as a way to reduce CPs' flying-hour shortage.

in Figures 4.1 to 4.3, the average number of pilots in a flight for a strategic airlifter (the C-5, C-141, and C-17) during the second half of the 1990s was 3.0 with 1.5 or more ACs. This implies that 50 percent of these flights would have two ACs in their aircrew. Replacing the second AC with a CP can thus generate many flying hours for CPs. However, wing commanders have other considerations in deciding whether to apply this measure. For example, wing commanders still consider C-17s to be new and C-17 CPs inexperienced. Moreover, a C-17 flight crew has neither a flight engineer nor a navigator. Therefore, even when the aircrew consists of three pilots, one more than the minimum, the combination of one AC and two CPs would be too risky for many missions. Moreover, wing commanders have already used only one AC and two CPs in about half of the C-17 flying hours and cannot increase that number much higher. Even for C-5s and C-141s, wing commanders prefer to have two ACs in the aircrew to handle complex missions despite the fact that there are two flight engineers on board. We believe that replacing the second AC with a CP is an attractive corrective measure that should be used whenever it does not affect flight safety.

Sixth, AMC has developed a new initiative, Channel Door to Door (CD2) or CAT B+,[6] in which AMC retains the option to use its airlifters for the flying segment between its APOEs and APODs. For the ground segment, AMC contracts CRAF participants to deliver cargo to the APOE and to send cargo from the APOD to the final destination. The aim of CD2 is to allow AMC to fly more whenever it needs to do so in order to meet its pilot training requirement. On the other hand, when the demand on AMC is high, it can use the Commercial Air Line of Communications (COMALOC) as a shock absorber to assume more deliveries. CD2 also attempts to be competitive with COMALOC in price and service quality. We support development of this program because it will give AMC more flexibility with which to meet fluctuating demand. The program commenced on October 1, 2001, and was expected to replace $10 million (or one-fifth) of all COMALOC buys during FY 2002.[7]

---

[6]Category B is a delivery service contracted for the full planeload, while Category A pertains to less than a full planeload. Traditionally, the commercial air carriers can provide service for both full and partial planeloads with door-to-door service while AMC cannot. CAT B+ takes advantage of both military airlift and commercial ground transportation to deliver less-than-full planeloads door to door.

[7]See *Air Committee Update*, Air Mobility Command, June 2001. Category A (commercial), which is carried through COMALOC, was estimated at $47 million. AMC wanted to transition part of these shipments to Germany and Korea to CD2 during FY 2002 and estimated the CD2 workload to be 22 percent of that of COMALOC during FY 2001. Assuming that the dollar value is proportional to workload, we arrived at $10 million for CD2.

In addition to CD2, AMC has been attempting to fold many of its air cargo tenders into the Military Air Line of Communications (MILALOC).[8] While a tender is not under TWCF, a MILALOC is. Commercial international tenders account for $25 million to $30 million per year, and retaining any part of those funds through MILALOC will result in more flying and revenue to AMC. On the other hand, to eliminate an annual organic flying-hour shortage of the size that appeared during FY 2000 and FY 2001, AMC would need to reduce commercial buys by an estimated $90 million, as indicated in Figure 8.1. CD2 and cutbacks in tenders, while beneficial and worthy of development, are insufficient to the task of eliminating the shortage.

Worse, the shortage may become even more severe from time to time because AMC will have more pilots.[9] Moreover, although AMC has taken measures to alleviate the flying-hour shortage, such measures can be expensive and, even when combined, are insufficient to resolve a severe shortage. We thus suggest that additional measures be implemented to help alleviate potential shortages.

Further Reduce the International Cargo Buy

In this section, we suggest corrective measures that can be immediately implemented to deal with the flying-hour shortage for CPs and with revenue loss. Measures that require a longer lead time before they can be implemented, as well as immediate and long-term measures to deal with problems other than these, are suggested in the section that follows.

Instead of flying with lighter payloads, AMC should further reduce its international cargo buys for channel and other missions. We suggest that AMC cut its international as opposed to domestic airlift buy. AMC seldom conducts domestic flights in any case. When substituting for commercial aircraft and airlift, organic strategic airlifters are more cost-effective in delivering cargo over a long distance and can generate more flying hours through international flights than through domestic flights. The international cargo buy—especially its expansion buy—has long been used as a flying-hour reservoir to provide additional flying hours to AMC pilots when needed. For the full fiscal year of 2001, AMC cut its international cargo buy by $77 million and retained the flying hours for organic aircraft. In fact, without factoring in post–September 11 activities, we estimated that the cut would have been $12 million higher, or $89 million.[10]

---

[8]Private communications with John Folkeson, RAND, March 11, 2002.

[9]See the section on insufficient flying hours in this chapter.

[10]The buy during September 2001 was $14.3 million, as opposed to $2.5 million during August. In other words, without the September 11 attacks, the buy would have been $12 million lower.

Because AMC cannot rely on any contingency to supply the needed flying hours, the question is, Without the September 11 attacks and without flying organic airlift with lighter loads, how many flying hours would AMC fall short during FY 2001? We estimated that just for the CPs of C-5s and C-17s, AMC would be short 11,800 hours, or 13 percent of its annual flying hours (in FY 2000). To eliminate the shortage for C-5 and C-17 CPs alone for a future year whose airlift demand is similar to that of FY 2001 (without September 11), AMC would need to cut $90 million from its already-reduced FY 2001 commercial cargo buy (see Figure 8.1). During FY 2001, the expansion buy was cut to merely $24.9 million from more than $100 million a year. It is unlikely to be cut much lower because even when airlift demand is generally low during the year, there are periods in which organic assets are overloaded and last-minute help from commercial carriers is needed. In such cases, the $90 million cut would have to come from the fixed buy and would amount to cutting that buy from $173 million to $83 million, or by half.[11]

Cutting the commercial buy can be less expensive than flying organic assets with lesser payloads. To demonstrate this, we need to compare the costs of the two alternatives. Alternative 1 involves flying organic assets more frequently but with lesser loads to generate additional flying hours for AMC pilots. This alternative amounts to flying organic assets by *N* additional hours without canceling any commercial buy to compensate. In terms of marginal cost involved in flying these extra *N* hours, it makes little difference whether AMC flies such hours with no cargo/passengers or with cargo/passengers diverted from originally planned organic flights.[12] Therefore, for the purpose of discussion, we assume that AMC flies those *N* hours empty in Alternative 1.

Alternative 2 is the same as Alternative 1 in that the organic assets are intended to fly the same additional *N* hours to reduce the flying-hour shortage by the same amount. The difference is that in Alternative 2, the *N* hours will be flown carrying as much cargo and passengers as the organic assets would allow. To further elaborate on this alternative, let this load be *L*. AMC is also planning to reduce its commercial buy by load *L* so that its organic and commercial assets together carry the same total load of cargo and passengers as before. There are two differences in marginal cost for the two alternatives. First, flying organic assets for *N* extra hours in Alternative 1 consumes less fuel than does Alternative 2 because an aircraft without a payload is lighter than one with a

---

[11]If AMC does not want to cut its fixed buy, we suggest that it cut its passenger expansion buy. See the next sectionfor more information.

[12]The latter spreads the cargo and passengers of originally planned trips into more trips, each with a lighter load. This can be an attractive approach if it is being implemented to make deliveries more timely. On the other hand, if the reason it is being implemented is to generate more flying hours for AMC pilots, as is shown here, spreading is not the least-cost alternative.

load. The second cost differential results from the cancellation of the commercial buy for carrying load *L* in Alternative 2.

By examining two extreme and opposite cases, we will show that reducing the commercial buy is less expensive than flying empty for both cases. In Case 1, we assume that in recent years CRAF participants have gained more business and profits and that their incentives to join CRAF have increased.[13] We further assume that these increased incentives are only partially canceled by the reduction in the annual commercial buy of load *L*. In this case, Alternative 2 is obviously less expensive than Alternative 1 because the former can save the fee that would otherwise have been paid to commercial carriers for delivering load *L*. This savings is far greater than the first cost differential, the fuel cost increment in carrying a load as opposed to no load.

In Case 2, the other extreme holds. A reduction in the annual commercial buy of load *L* will make incentives for CRAF participation no longer adequate because existing incentives were barely sufficient before the cut. AMC must then compensate the commercial carriers so that their profit is the same whether they deliver load *L* or not. The original fee that was to be paid to the commercial carriers for carrying load *L* can be divided into three components: avoidable variable cost, unavoidable variable cost, and profit. To make the commercial carriers indifferent to Alternatives 1 and 2 in terms of profit and incentives, AMC need only pay those carriers the last two components but not the first. For example, the fuel cost in flying load *L* belongs to the avoidable variable cost. The aging and depreciation of the aircraft caused by the additional flights for the delivery of load *L* are also part of the avoidable variable cost. Part of the flight-crew cost in flying the aircraft and of the labor and material cost in servicing these aircraft during and after their flights to bring them back to preflight conditions can also be avoidable cost.[14] It is now clear that the avoidable variable cost is a significant fraction of the fee and that the unavoidable variable cost and the profit combined are still considerably smaller than the fee.

---

[13]This is a possible case. The annual value of commercial augmentation in constant 1999 dollars during peacetime (excluding 1990–1991 and 1994) has increased 11 percent between 1981 and 1999. Moreover, there are a host of new businesses in which only CRAF members can participate. These businesses include the $1.5 billion City Pairs Program for federal government passengers' domestic and international air travel; the Express Small Package Program for domestic air delivery; and WWX. There are also tenders, DVD, and Premium Service. (See Chapter Six for details on these businesses.) Although through the years CRAF has been required to provide an increasing airlift capability, we believe it is quite possible that the incentives for CRAF participation would remain sufficient even following the reduction of the commercial buy for load *L*.

[14]One can argue that canceling the flights for load *L* would not allow the commercial carriers to recoup all of the variable labor costs for the flight and ground crew because this crew would already have been hired and scheduled to fly and service those flights. However, placing a lower commercial buy before the start of a fiscal year instead of canceling at the last minute might give enough warning to commercial carriers of lower demand and help them avoid part of the variable labor cost.

In sum, the whole fee is paid to commercial carriers for carrying the additional load *L* in Alternative 1, but only the unavoidable variable cost and profit need be paid in Alternative 2. Thus, Alternative 2 is less expensive in both extreme cases and is likely to be less costly in all other intermediate cases as well.

AMC should reduce its international cargo expansion and fixed buy from commercial carriers to compensate for the additional organic flying it needs. It should, however, estimate the overall incentives for CRAF participation to ensure that this reduction does not exceed recent incentive increases and does not lead to any CRAF withdrawal. Otherwise, AMC should pay commercial carriers a fraction of the fee that would have been charged for carrying load *L* to compensate carriers for their loss of business in delivering load *L*. One plausible scheme is for AMC to pay commercial carriers their unavoidable variable costs and typical profits, but not their full fees, on those fixed buys that are canceled during the fiscal year. On the other hand, there will be no compensation to commercial carriers on expansion buys that are anticipated but do not materialize. Expansion buys are last-minute buys, and commercial carriers already know that AMC has no obligation to issue any or all of them.

In sum, whether paying none or a fraction of the fee, AMC will find this alternative less expensive than flying organic assets more frequently and with lesser loads.

Add an Organic, Dedicated Passenger-Carrying Capability

As shown in Figure 8.1, the international cargo buy, which has previously served as a flying-hour reservoir, can run low when AMC uses it to retain sufficient organic flying. Worse, circumstances can exacerbate the flying-hour shortage to the point at which even exhausting this reservoir will not suffice. For example, AMC has decided to buy 60 C-17s in addition to the 120 it has already authorized.[15] These additional aircraft will likely necessitate more pilots and hence more flying hours during peacetime to keep those pilots trained. We suggest that AMC create another flying-hour reservoir from the international passenger buy.

The international passenger buy has remained at about $350 million a year in spite of severe cuts in the international cargo buy (see Figure 8.2).[16] Table 8.1

[15]This study does not suggest that a smaller number of additional C-17s should be acquired. The decision on C-17s is based on many factors. This study merely identifies the implications for flying hours during peacetime so that any negative ramifications can be corrected.

[16]Like the international cargo buy, the international passenger buy is in CAT B, which is the buy for the full planeload.

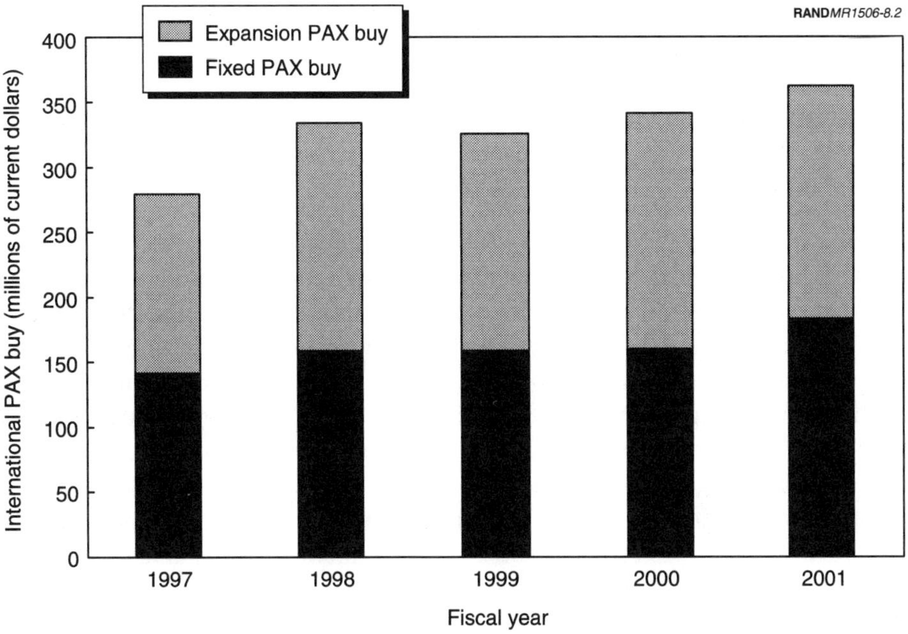

Figure 8.2—AMC Did Not Reduce Its International Passenger Buy Despite Insufficient Flying

Table 8.1

Passenger Buys Carry a Sizable Number of Passengers per Trip

Mission	Size of Buy (millions of dollars)	Passengers Delivered	Trips	Passengers per Trip
Channel	194.08	207,585	705	294
Contingency	74.37	83,480	296	282
Exercise	49.32	61,589	195	316
Special assignment airlifr missions	41.34	46,785	162	289
Total	359.11	399,439	1,358	1,181

SOURCE: Annual data for FY 2001 from International Airlift—Contract FY 2001, AMC/DOY.

shows that regardless of the mission type, the average number of passengers per trip is sizable, approaching 300. If the number were much smaller, AMC would have to fly frequent trips and incur high expenses in order to provide the same service in house. With so many trips of near-full planeloads, AMC has an opportunity to economically fly some of these trips when it needs more flying for pilot training. Unfortunately, AMC does not yet have an organic capability dedicated to carrying planeloads of passengers. Therefore, before the international passenger buy can be cut, AMC must develop an organic, dedicated passenger-carrying capability so that its organic assets can deliver the passengers who were originally to be carried on commercial flights. Instead of acquiring passenger aircraft, AMC would find it much cheaper to obtain a conversion set that could convert an airlifter or a tanker from carrying cargo to carrying passengers exclusively. This set could be designed so that it could be installed and uninstalled quickly.

AMC has been considering the possibility of purchasing palletized seats for 34 C-17s and storing them for wartime use. Although these seats are currently not intended for peacetime applications, they should be thus designated, as their peacetime use does not preclude their use in war, and it would be most cost-effective to employ them at all times. In peacetime, such seats could generate much needed flying hours. In wartime, there would no longer be a lack of organic flying hours, so the seats could be used not for generating flying hours but rather for their originally intended wartime missions. With the palletized seats that AMC is considering, each C-17 could accommodate 134 passengers.[17] We estimate that a conversion set based on these palletized seats, and with the addition of pallets for baggage storage and lavatories, would cost about $300,000. Moreover, because a 134-passenger capacity is well below 294, the average number of passengers carried per trip by the chartered commercial carriers (see Table 8.1), AMC should be able to replace some of these chartered flights with filled C-17s.

We also estimate that to eliminate the shortage of 8700 flying hours for C-17 CPs,[18] a dozen C-17s would have to fly the same number of flying hours carrying passengers. The capital outlay for a dozen C-17 conversion sets would be only $3.6 million. AMC would then be able to reduce its international passenger buy by $50 million a year and fly those passengers with the organic converted passenger carriers.[19] The income (revenue net of expenses) earned by AMC in just one year would exceed this $3.6 million outlay. Moreover, if AMC decided to buy palletized seats for 34 C-17s for other purposes but agreed to use a dozen of them to carry passengers during peacetime, the $3.6 million would be a sunk cost that should not be double-counted toward peacetime applications. In any case, the conversion would be cost-effective in that it

[17]See "C-17 Centerline Palletized Tourist Class Seating Configuration," Cadillac, MI: AAR Cadillac Manufacturing, November 21, 2000.

[18]The shortage was discussed earlier in this chapter.

[19]We do not suggest that AMC take back the bulk of the $350 million for the international passenger buys as shown in Figure 8.2 because AMC's route structure is different from that of the commercial air carriers and cannot provide the same frequency of services. However, because Table 8.1 shows that these buys carry close to 300 passengers per trip regardless of the mission type, it would be quite feasible for AMC to retain $50 million or more of business for its organic flying.

would allow the strategic airlifters to generate both flying hours and revenue at the same time, as opposed to flying empty simply to generate flying hours.[20]

We can improve the cost-effectiveness of these measures even further by advocating the use of KC-10s instead of C-17s as dedicated passenger carriers. Because C-17s are better suited than KC-10s to carrying cargo, it would be more efficient for AMC to retain C-17s for cargo-carrying purposes. Moreover, KC-10s have a larger capacity for carrying passengers than do C-17s. The KC-10 is derived from the DC-10, a passenger carrier. Its wings are at the bottom, and the floor level where seats are installed is closer to the diameter of the fuselage and is thus wider, thereby accommodating more seats abreast. The preliminary design of the KC-10 further indicates that it can seat over 200 passengers[21]—more than the 134 accommodated by the current C-17 conversion design. However, a KC-10 conversion set could cost twice as much as that associated with the C-17 because an oxygen system might have to be installed in each seat and because there will be a higher cost for more palletized seats. However, even $600,000 is a small quantity compared with the annual revenue and income the KC-10 could generate.

KC-10s currently fly 5000 hours per year for cargo delivery. AMC should switch this cargo flying to C-17s and let KC-10s spend those 5000 hours carrying passengers instead. This switch would generate more revenue than would be the case if KC-10s were used to carry cargo and C-17s to carry passengers.

In an earlier study,[22] we found that an organic, dedicated passenger-carrying capability is needed during wartime. Potential adversaries such as Iraq and North Korea can now attack airfields with chemical or biological weapons. Even conventional munitions carried by ballistic missiles or special operations forces can prevent CRAF aircraft from landing at airfields in the theater.[23] After

[20]For those who are concerned that AMC will not be able to economically retain $50 million worth of international passenger buy, we reiterate that AMC can convert a smaller number of C-17s for the smaller amount of traffic it projects. Because the conversion cost is proportional to the number of C-17s to be converted, the lower gain in anticipated business would not make the conversion uneconomical. It would, however, reduce the total amount of cost savings in the conversion.

[21]The KC-10's commercial counterpart, the DC-10, can carry up to 380 passengers. However, a converted KC-10 would carry less because KC-10s do not have cargo compartments in the bottom of the fuselage for passenger luggage and equipment; this space is taken instead by fuel tanks. Thus, some space in the converted KC-10 must be reserved for holding these items.

[22]RAND October 2001 research.

[23]For example, Major James Hanley found that "the U.S. currently does not provide adequate measures to defend all the airlift forces against man-portable surface-to-air missiles during humanitarian relief missions." (See James Hanley, "Force Protection of Strategic Airlift Forces in the Operations Other than War Environment," Fort Leavenworth, KS: School of Advanced Military Studies, United States Army Command and General Staff College, May 21, 1998, p. iii.) This study was done in 1995. Since then, the threat would only have increased. Moreover, the threat could also be much more severe in major contingencies as opposed to humanitarian missions.

the first Scud missiles were fired during the Gulf War, for example, several major commercial air carriers refused to permit flights into the area at night, when most of the Scud missile attacks occurred.[24] The Scud attacks also caused volunteerism to drop in some companies. In some cases, management flew missions because fewer crew members were willing to fly into threatened airfields.[25] During the Gulf War, 78 percent of all air cargo landed at five APODs.[26] Because a disruption at even one or two APODs would have affected the war effort, APOD attacks are lucrative and are likely to be used in future contingencies.

CRAF, being unequipped and untrained for protection, might not be able or willing to land at airfields that are vulnerable to attacks. We have thus proposed a transload approach in which CRAF aircraft would stop at safe airfields closest to the theater. In the Korean contingency, with both South Korea and Japan under ballistic missile threat, the closest safe airfields suitable for massive strategic air mobility operations may be at Guam. Shuttling passengers between Guam and APODs in South Korea requires converted strategic, as opposed to tactical, airlifters or tankers. The cargo and passengers carried by CRAF would be reloaded at the transload airfields onto organic aircraft, which would continue onto threatened airfields in the theater. To fill this need, AMC would require dedicated, organic passenger-carrying aircraft, which it currently lacks. Moreover, civil aircraft were grounded immediately after September 11 terrorist attacks. If AMC had large, dedicated passenger-carrying aircraft, it could use them for urgent travel, including the delivery of rescue personnel. However, the key peacetime justification for such aircraft remains the need for a second flying-hour reservoir (in addition to the existing one based on carrying cargo). Thus, there are multiple wartime and peacetime justifications for developing a passenger-carrying capability.

Make Nonpaying Passengers Pay

Military service personnel and their dependents currently fly free on military flights and AMC-chartered commercial flights when empty seats are available. While we would not dispute the fact that filling empty seats is a much deserved fringe benefit for service personnel and their dependents, we believe that this

---

[24]See John Lund, Ruth Berg, and Corinne Replogle, *Project AIR FORCE Analysis of the Air War in the Gulf: An Assessment of Strategic Airlift Operational Efficiency*, R-4269/4-AF, Santa Monica: RAND, 1993, p. 29.

[25]See Chenoweth, *The Civil Reserve Air Fleet and Operation Desert Shield/Desert Storm: Issues for the Future*, MR-298-AF, Santa Monica: RAND, 1993, p. 49.

[26]See Defense Science Board, *Report of the Defense Science Board Task Force on Strategic Mobility*, August 15, 1996, p. 56.

benefit should be borne by the individual services, not solely by AMC. We would thus propose that nonpaying passengers be charged a fare of, say, $100 on average per one-way trip. If the services reimbursed their personnel and dependents, the load factor would be unchanged, and AMC would receive $24 million a year.[27] Even if nonpaying passengers had to pay the fare themselves, the load factor would not be greatly affected, and the same $24 million could accrue to AMC because most of these flights are overseas trips for which the $100 fare is still a bargain. If the discounted seats were sold to nonmilitary government personnel as well, the load factor and revenue could further increase.

Moreover, a recent study reported that "there is a great deal of organic airlift capacity that is going unused while commanders are spending precious travel dollars to move their people on commercial flights."[28] AMC should adjust prices and communicate and negotiate with commanders and government customers for better utilization of the unused capacity.

Decide Whether to Allow AMC Limited Participation in Commercial Air Delivery`

Traditionally, AMC has not been involved in commercial business. However, the need to conduct cost-effective air mobility operations for national security justifies AMC's limited participation in the commercial air delivery of cargo and passengers.

AMC often flies organic assets partially or totally empty, particularly during return flights. It would help AMC financially if the command were allowed to deliver commercial cargo and passengers for a fee whenever its organic or chartered commercial flights were not full. Because of AMC's route structure and service-quality considerations, we do not anticipate that the commercial airlift industry will lose much business to AMC. To ensure that this is the case, the U.S. government can set an upper limit on the amount of commercial business AMC can undertake. For example, $100 million or $200 million might be a suitable limit. This revenue, in conjunction with other corrective measures, could then be used to eliminate the flying-hour shortage.

AMC should examine its route structure and its competitiveness to determine where and how often it can offer commercial services on its existing flights. On the other hand, letting the military participate in commerce, even if highly re-

---

[27]As shown in Figure 6.4, military flights carried 132,000 nonpaying passengers, and AMC-chartered commercial flights carried another 110,000, during FY 1999.

[28]See Captain Christopher Pike, "Duty Passenger Travel: Education and Analysis," Air University, Wright-Patterson Air Force Base, Ohio, AFIT/GMO/LAL/98J-13, June 1998, p. ii.

stricted, is a drastic step both politically and philosophically. We do not recommend such a program at this time. Rather, the government should estimate the program's benefit and decide whether AMC should be allowed to participate in the commercial air delivery business in such a restricted manner.

Competitively Price Organic Services

Competitiveness requires that organic airlift services be priced appropriately against comparable commercial services and that organic services be run in a cost-effective manner so that these prices can be sustained without increasing subsidies to AMC. Staying competitive would have two key advantages. First, customers would have fewer incentives to bypass AMC and seek airlift services elsewhere. A stable customer base would help AMC generate enough flying hours for its own pilots. Second, even with competitive pricing, AMC would continue to incur an annual loss for its operations because it has large but legitimate "war readiness" costs that commercial air carriers do not. The change in this annual operating loss over time would become an effective measure of cost containment and quality improvement,[29] with a reduction in annual loss pointing to more efficient operations. AMC needs such an objective measure to improve the cost-effectiveness of its operations.

Some might favor an opposite system, maintaining that the main purpose of owning organic assets and personnel is to allow AMC to provide airlift services to the military during crisis or war. This argument holds that the peacetime activities necessary for training and maintaining readiness prevent AMC from competing with commercial air carriers on the basis of price and quality. Consequently, if the choice of service is decided by free-market forces, AMC's customers will prefer commercial over organic services, and AMC will lose business. If this argument were valid, we would suggest converting TWCF to a credit system. On the basis of historic usage and future trends, AMC would allocate each military customer credits for passenger and cargo delivery during a given fiscal year. These credits would expire within the fiscal year and would be nontransferable. Customers would then seek to use these credits for organic services before turning to commercial air carriers. AMC would be guaranteed a certain number of flying hours that would not vary from those planned and would use those hours for pilot training and aging purposes. The drawback of the credit system is its nonmarket mechanism. Although AMC would have full control of those flying hours, it would lose its best objective measure, the competitive airlift market, to assess how well it improves the cost-effectiveness of its

[29]The operating loss should be adjusted for changes beyond AMC's control, such as higher "war readiness" costs due to higher wartime requirements.

air mobility operations. We therefore do not consider the credit system to be of long-term interest to AMC.

Let us now return to competitive pricing. The objective of AMC, as the executive agent for the air mobility forces, should be to meet peacetime demand and to maintain wartime readiness at the lowest cost to the U.S. government. When AMC uses commercial augmentation, it can often lower the cost of meeting demand but not necessarily the cost of maintaining readiness. For example, when commercial air carriers assume too many missions, AMC ends up creating extra nonreimbursable missions specifically for training purposes. The full cost of these training missions would be more than the partial cost of subsidizing corresponding reimbursable missions, which generate the same number of flying hours for training. A key question, then, is how to price the organic services.

The principle underlying the TWCF is for AMC "to finance the operating costs of the airlift services provided by AMC, which is reimbursed for such costs by authorized customers to whom airlift services are rendered."[30] Under this principle, cost reimbursement plays a central role in the pricing scheme for organic airlift services. TWCF planners were concerned from the start that its prices were too high to be competitive. Instead of simply setting market-competitive prices, however, they eliminated various cost components, such as military pay and of the acquisition and depreciation of property and capital equipment associated with the airlift,[31] so that the reimbursable costs or the prices charged to AMC customers could be lower and thus competitive. Unfortunately, since its establishment in 1958, TWCF has had continuing difficulties in deciding which cost components to include for reimbursement as well as in setting prices so that it can break even on an annual basis. This breakeven approach has a problem in addition to the difficulty in hitting the breakeven point every year: When there is a choice between competitiveness and achieving the breakeven point, the latter wins. If AMC is not competitive, however, it can lose customers to commercial air carriers.[32] This is one reason the commercial TWCF is increasing.

Fortunately, USTRANSCOM and the Defense Logistics Agency, in coordination with the military services, in February 2000 established the Strategic

---

[30]See *Command Data Book*, November 1999, p. 144.

[31]See Colonel James True and William Nawyn, *The Airlift Service Industrial Fund 1958–1988: The Evolution of an Effective Management Approach*, Scott Air Force Base, IL: Military Airlift Command, Office of History, February 1989, p. 7.

[32]Under the breakeven approach, AMC can still examine the trend, over the years, of whether more or fewer cost components are included and use the inclusion as a measure of its competitiveness. The fewer cost components that are included to break even, the less competitive AMC is.

Distribution Management Initiative (SDMI)—an effort that aims to improve DoD's end-to-end distribution system by balancing customer service, cost, readiness, and sustainability. Early results have already shown significant reduction in customer wait time. The first SDMI pilot began in Europe in July 2000. The wait time for air delivery of sustainment cargo to Bosnia has been reduced from 15.0 days to 10.7 days, representing a 29 percent reduction. In addition, on April 16, 2001, USTRANSCOM began a test of shifting 17 pallets per week from commercial air service to military air for three locations in Germany: Baumholder, Kitzingen, and Schweinfurt. Early analysis indicated that the resulting wait time is matching and often beating commercial performance. USTRANSCOM has also "adjusted organic rates to mirror commercial practice."[33] It is thus clear that USTRANSCOM is using commercial performance and prices as metrics and that the quality of its service can be improved significantly. We recommend, however, that USTRANSCOM and AMC go further along the lines suggested here.

For example, the desire to minimize subsidies and maximize reimbursements to organic services has led to different prices for different categories of customers. The per-hour rates for channel passengers, channel cargo, and special airlift are lowest for DoD users, intermediate for non-DoD other-U.S.-government users, and highest for non-U.S.-government users.[34] The justification for charging different prices for the same service is to "comply with national policy to recover costs incurred when supporting non-DoD and non-U.S.-government activities."[35] A pricing scheme based on subsidy and cost recovery is not competitive pricing. When an organic service is priced higher than the market price, customers have an incentive to shun AMC and seek a commercial provider. There are already avenues for AMC customers to bypass AMC. When its services are priced lower, AMC receives less revenue to support its air mobility operations. AMC should charge all the customers the same price for the same service, and the price should be competitive.

When determining competitive prices for organic services that AMC wants to keep in house, AMC need not consider the cost of the service or the amount of

---

[33]See "Strategic Distribution Management Initiative Under Way," USTRANSCOM News Service, July 6, 2001.

[34]Passenger and cargo channel rates can be found in *U.S. Government Department of Defense (DoD) Airlift Rates, U.S. Government Non-Department of Defense (Non-DoD) Rate Tariffs*, and *Non-U.S. Government and FMS Tariffs*, Scott Air Force Base, IL: Headquarters Air Mobility Command FMBT, October 17, 2000. Special airlift rates can be found in *Charters—Special Assignment Airlift Missions (SAAMs), Joint Chiefs of Staff Exercises (JCSE), Contingencies for the Transportation Working Capital Fund (TWCF)*, and *Non-TWCF Aircraft*, Scott Air Force Base, IL: Headquarters Air Mobility Command/FMBT, October 17, 2000, and in the *Command Data Book*, November 1999, p. 78.

[35]*Command Data Book*, November 1999, p. 78.

subsidy and should charge the market price for the same service, adjusted for the service quality differential. A competitive market-based pricing scheme[36] has the advantage of clearly demonstrating the true worth of a particular peacetime organic service.

AMC may not want to compete in certain services and may seek instead to outsource such services to commercial providers when the costs of providing the services exceed the competitive prices it can charge. On the other hand, AMC should price certain airlift services competitively even if its reimbursements do not fully cover its marginal expenses. Offering certain services that afford valuable training experience with only partial reimbursement is better than arranging dedicated training missions without any reimbursement at all.

Competitive pricing also means that AMC can charge customers a much higher price to recoup the full cost (both fixed and variable) for unique and valuable services such as airlifting outsize cargo unsuited to commercial carriers. This is an avenue for increasing airlift revenue to AMC to support its operations.

AMC should charge a single competitive price for the same service, eliminating the price differential among the current three categories of customers: DoD, non-DoD U.S., and non-U.S. Otherwise, if one price is the competitive price, the other two cannot be. Charging more than the competitive price could drive customers away, and charging less results in less money flowing to AMC to support its operations.

To stay competitive, AMC should also lower prices for services that are inferior in terms of on-time delivery or passenger comfort. At the same time, however, lower prices will result in even lower revenue to AMC, and inferior services will drive customers away. Thus, lowering prices alone is not a viable strategy for remaining competitive. Recognizing the implications of poor services, AMC has started programs such as SDMI to improve service, and the results thus far have been promising. Both competitive pricing and competitive service are the goals for which AMC airlift operations should aim.

If AMC switches to a competitive pricing scheme, one should expect a one-time change, or even decline, of the TWCF flowing to AMC. This bookkeeping change will not, however, affect the total cost of AMC operations to the U.S. government. If the transition causes a decline in the TWCF, a compensating increase should be added to the O&M fund. The current trend is a declining TWCF share, but it should improve once the transition to competitive pricing is

[36]Although AMC is not equipped to adjust its prices in near real time, it can use averaged market prices, adjusted for quality differentials, for airlift services that it wants to keep in house. By this means, customers would have much less incentive to bypass AMC and give airlift business to commercial air carriers.

complete. Such pricing should help keep customers from diverting business from AMC. In addition, the new pricing should give AMC a clearer picture of whether its service quality is improving and its costs are declining.

DEALING WITH PROBLEMS OTHER THAN THE FLYING-HOUR SHORTAGE AND REVENUE LOSS

The measures described above will not only alleviate the flying-hour shortage and revenue loss but also ease other problems, as described below.

Congress Should Allow AMC to Vary the Number of Authorized Pilots

We found that the total number of actual CPs for both airlifters (the C-5s, C-141s, C-17s, and C-130s) and tankers (the KC-135s and KC-10s) has exceeded the authorized number since 1986, exhibiting an upward trend. However, this deviation was greatly reduced in FY 2001. The actual number of CPs during FY 2001 exceeded the authorized number by only 49 out of a total of 948, and the number of ACs exceeded that authorized by 29 out of a total of 949. The salary savings that would result from eliminating these positions would be about $5.1 million per year.[37] This is not a very large savings considering the havoc to morale that would result if these pilots were reassigned or laid off. Congress should thus allow AMC some flexibility in deviating from the number of pilots authorized as long as AMC makes compensatory adjustments in other budgetary items to keep its overall operational expenses within the bounds of congressional authorizations.

Congress Should Formally Allow AMC to Vary the Mix of Authorized Copilots and Aircraft Commanders

In FY 2001, the actual CP/AC ratios of the airlifters (the C-5s, C-141s, C-17s, and C-130s) were above the authorized ratios, while those of the tankers (the KC-135s and KC-10s) were below. Where the actual ratios of airlifters exceeded authorized ratios, reducing the ratios to those authorized would have amounted to replacing 66 CPs with ACs, in which case salary costs would have risen by $1 million. On the other hand, a CP is required to fly many more hours

[37]This amount was calculated on the basis of the following data: For CPs, the average grade is captain and the average duration of service is about six years; for ACs, the average grade is major and the average duration of service is 11 years. (See *Command Data Book*, November 1999, p. 49.) Further, the annual regular military compensation (basic pay, basic allowance for housing, and basic allowance for subsistence and the federal tax advantage on the tax-free allowance) would be $60,591 for an average CP and $75,227 for an AC. (See *2001 Uniformed Services Almanac*, Falls Church, VA: Uniformed Services Almanac, Inc., 2001.)

per month than is an AC. When flying-hour shortages recur, replacing 66 CPs with ACs could significantly reduce the flying hours needed. The marginal flying cost for just one hour per month for 66 CPs would be $2.7 million,[38] which would exceed the $1 million annual salary cost cited above. AMC thus has financial incentives to reduce the actual CP/AC ratios for airlifters to those authorized if flying-hour shortages recur often.

For tankers, whose actual ratios were below those authorized, the salary savings in making actual ratios the same as those authorized is equivalent to $800,000 a year. However, just one extra flying hour per month for all of the 55 additional CPs would amount to $2.1 million, which exceeds the salary savings of $800,000. Therefore, if AMC is allowed to keep the actual ratios for the tankers from equaling those authorized, it should not be tempted to replace ACs with CPs for the small salary savings. The added flying-hour requirement and cost for the switch from ACs to CPs would be much too high whenever a flying-hour shortage occured.

Instead of generally not enforcing the authorized mix of CPs and ACs, Congress should formally allow AMC to vary the mix as long as the variation does not increase its total authorized operational expenses, including salaries and training. AMC is in a better position than Congress to optimize this mix.

Flying-Hour Shortage Corrective Measures Would Increase Piloting During Training

We have found an undesirable trend of less piloting during training. Once the suggested measures ensure that AMC has plentiful flying hours even during periods of low airlift demand, this problem can be resolved by reducing the number of pilots per flight so that each will have more opportunities to pilot as opposed to observing others piloting.

Reduce and Adapt to Deviations from the Flying Plan

During the 1990s, the actual flying hours for airlifters deviated increasingly from the flying plan. Making last-minute adjustments in the flight schedule can be difficult and costly for AMC in assembling needed aircraft and personnel in a hurry. Pilots' quality of life can also be lowered by short-notice flights. This increased deviation was caused by the transition from the Cold War to the post–Cold War era, and thus it is quite possible that the trend will not continue. To

---

[38]To arrive at $2.7 million, we used the costs per aircraft flying hour for various airlifters appearing in the *Command Data Book*, November 1999, pp. 77–78. See also Chapter Three.

reduce the deviation, however, AMC should improve its projection capability to include a more frequent update of its flying plan. It can also reduce commercial fixed buys and increase commercial expansion buys in its plan for the fiscal year. When AMC is running short on flying hours during the fiscal year, it can reduce its expansion buys, which AMC has not yet issued, and thus fly more for the remainder of the year. Equally important, AMC should accept deviation as a viable means of training, as war can also come with short notice.

Contract Out and Adapt to More Engagement Missions

For airlifters, engagement missions, which are typically for short-notice small-scale contingencies, have accounted for an increasing share of organic flying hours. It is quite likely that this trend will level off, albeit at a higher share of engagement missions than that seen during the Cold War era. Again, a two-pronged approach, as suggested in the subsection above, should be used. First, AMC should improve its projection and use more commercial expansion, instead of fixed, buys. Second, AMC should see a larger number of engagement missions as opportunities to train for quick-response operations.

Recommended Measures Would Increase Reimbursement for Training

Competitive pricing and better services will help AMC retain customers and halt the decline in the reimbursable share of its operating and training expenses. Competitive pricing adjusted for service quality establishes clear goals for AMC to reduce costs and retain business. Moreover, once AMC makes equitable arrangements with commercial air carriers for reduced commercial buys when flying-hour shortages occur and uses its dedicated, passenger-carrying capability for new business, it can retain more reimbursable cargo and passenger business in house.

TOWARD COST-EFFECTIVE AIR MOBILITY OPERATIONS

Peacetime demand continues to exhibit wide fluctuation. Not only can demand be high, but it can also be too low to provide the necessary flying hours for pilot training. Moreover, the wartime requirement for air mobility is on the rise, generating more asymmetry in both wartime and peacetime demand. This asymmetry makes a flying-hour shortage even more likely, as a larger number of pilots needed for wartime will require more flying hours for training during peacetime. Although AMC has been taking action to gain flexibility in meeting fluctuating airlift demand during peacetime, we have proposed additional corrective measures for generating new business and more flying for AMC when shortages recur as well as for gaining flexibility in using and not using commercial air carriers to smooth the demand for organic assets. These measures also include some that would make AMC services more competitive with the commercial services, thereby stemming the loss of business from AMC. These corrective measures should help AMC meet peacetime demand and maintain wartime readiness in a cost-effective manner.

Appendix

ADDITIONAL GRAPHS SHOWING VARIOUS ASPECTS OF PEACETIME AIR MOBILITY OPERATIONS

The graphs in this appendix provide added support to various statements made in the main text. For example, examining the operations of AMC's organic assets was the main task of this study. When we analyzed a particular aspect of these assets' operations, however, we generally showed only the graph of the C-5 while discussing the characteristics and trends of all aircraft in the main text. We then referred the reader to corresponding graphs in this appendix for aircraft other than those shown in the text.

STRATEGIC AIRLIFT CAPACITY

Figures A.1 and A.2 show the decline of strategic airlift capacity since 1992, whether the capacity was measured according to Air Force planning factors or Gulf War experience. This issue was discussed in Chapter Two.

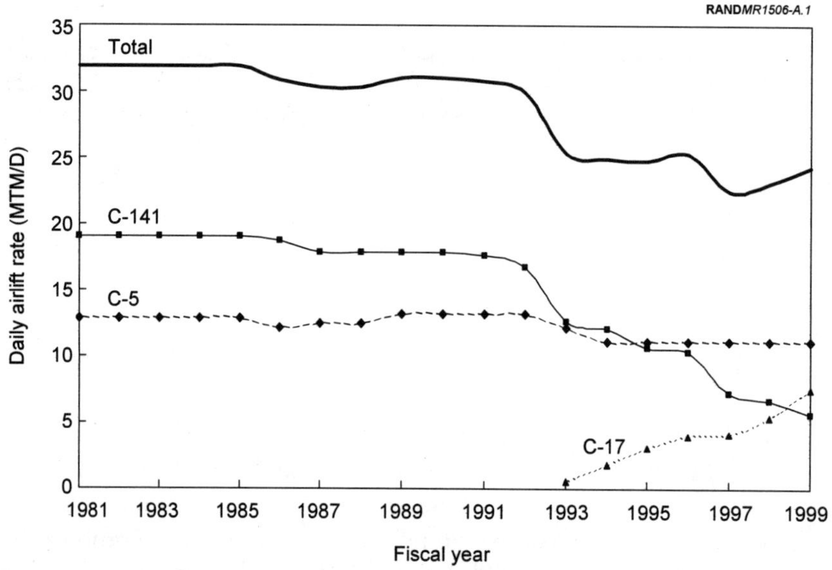

Figure A.1—Strategic Airlift Capacity Has Dropped Since 1992 (capacity based on Air Force planning factors)

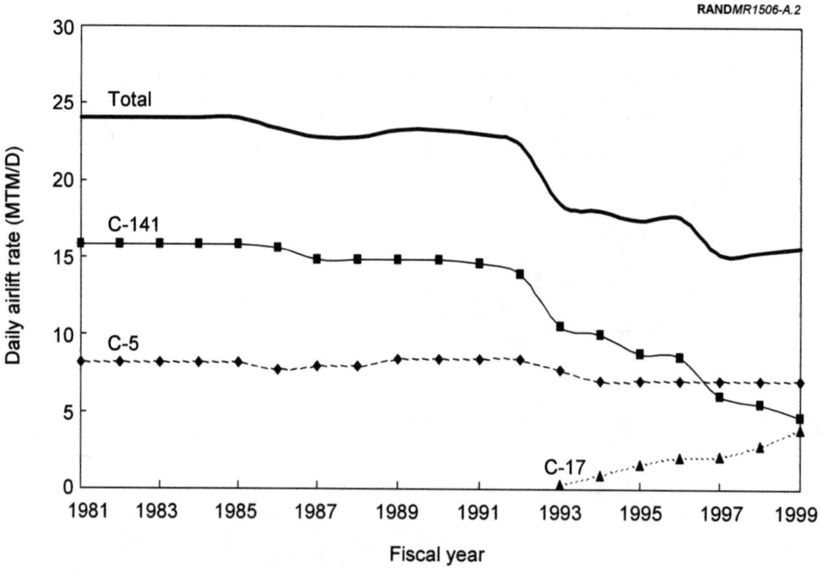

Figure A.2—Strategic Airlift Capacity Has Dropped Since 1992 (capacity based on Gulf War experience)

U.S. MILITARY INSTALLATIONS AND PERSONNEL ABROAD

Figures A.3 and A.4 show that U.S. military involvement overseas declined sharply after the Cold War, as discussed in Chapter Two.

ANNUAL AIRCRAFT INVENTORY

Figure A.5 shows the annual aircraft inventory of the six organic aircraft described in Chapter Two.

ANNUAL FLYING HOURS PER AIRCRAFT

Figures A.6 to A.10 show annual flying hours per aircraft during peacetime for the C-14, C-17, C-130, KC-135, and KC-10, as discussed in Chapter Two. Data for the C-5 appear in the main text as Figure 2.6.

C-130s were transferred to the Air Combat Command during FY 1993 and back to AMC during FY 1997. Consequently, some of the data points during the 1990s are not included in the C-130 figures throughout the report because data under different commands may not be comparable.

RANDMR1506-A.3

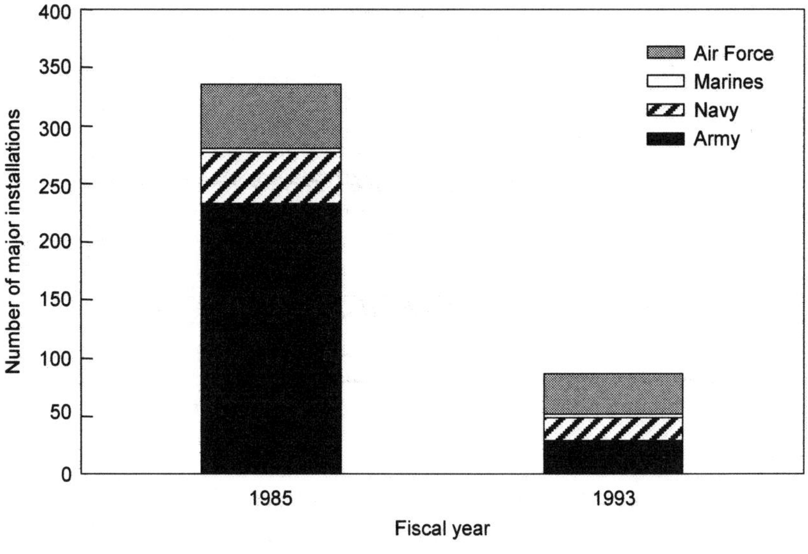

SOURCE: Based on data from the *Department of Defense Fact Book*, Washington, D.C.: U.S. Department of Defense, January 1985 and January 1994.

Figure A.3—U.S. Military Installations Abroad Declined Rapidly After the Cold War

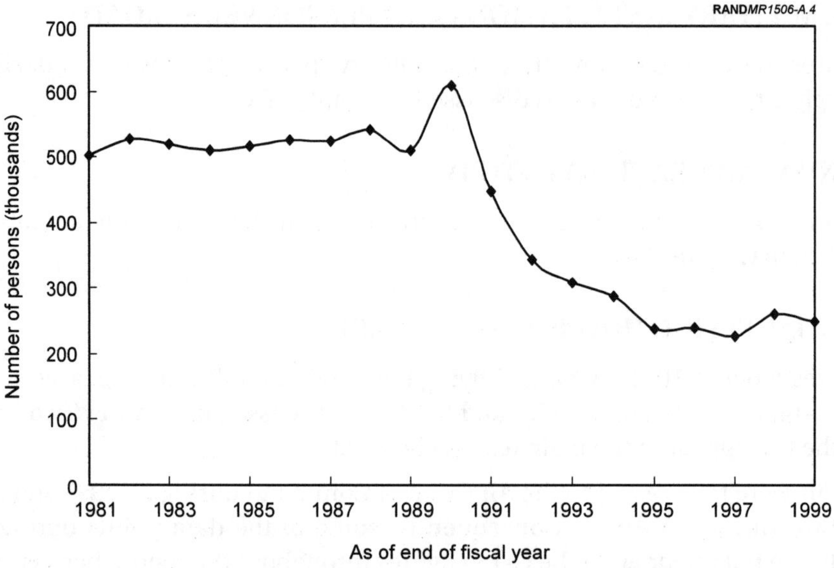

SOURCE: Based on data from the *Statistical Abstract of the United States*, Washington, D.C.: Government Printing Office, 1990, 1991, and 2000.

Figure A.4—Military Active-Duty Personnel Abroad Declined Rapidly After the Cold War

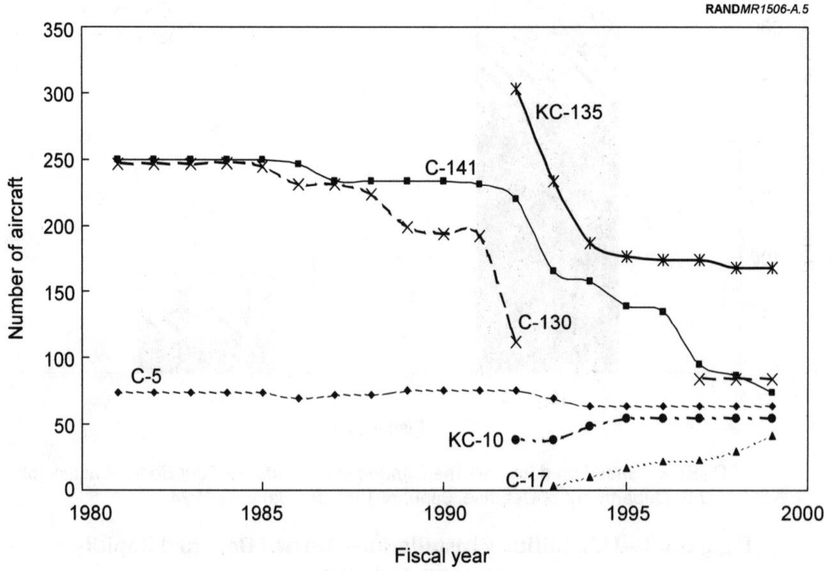

Figure A.5—Annual Aircraft Inventory

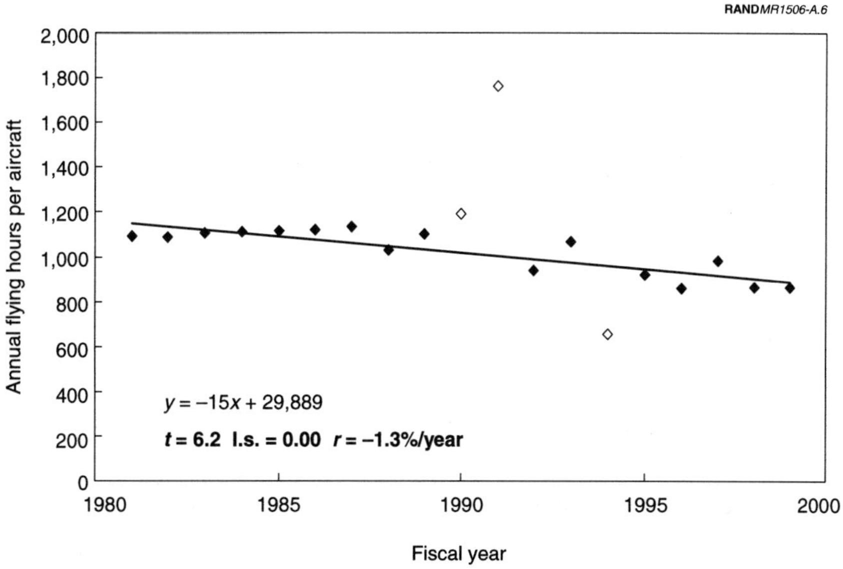

NOTE: Data points for 1990, 1991, and 1994 were excluded from the determination of the trend line.

Figure A.6—C-141 Annual Flying Hours per Aircraft During Peacetime

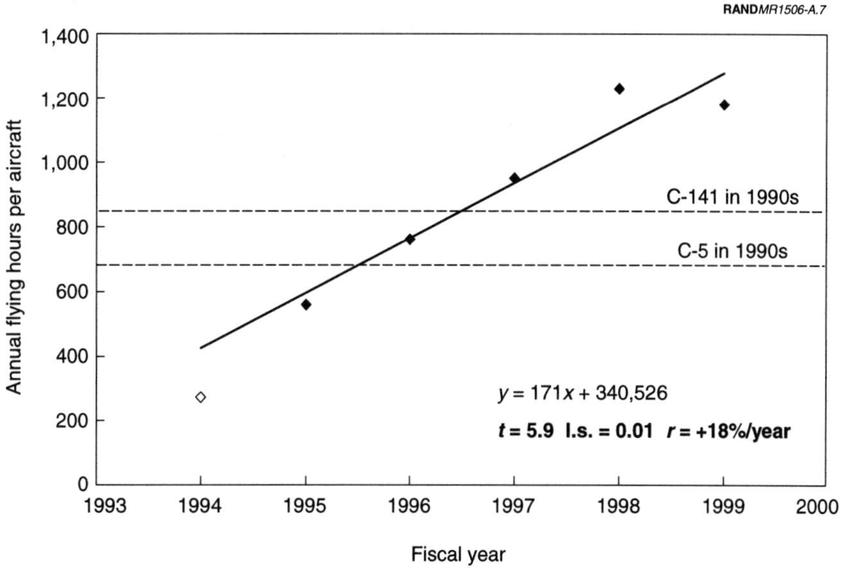

NOTE: The data point for 1994 was excluded from the determination of the trend line.

Figure A.7—C-17 Annual Flying Hours per Aircraft During Peacetime

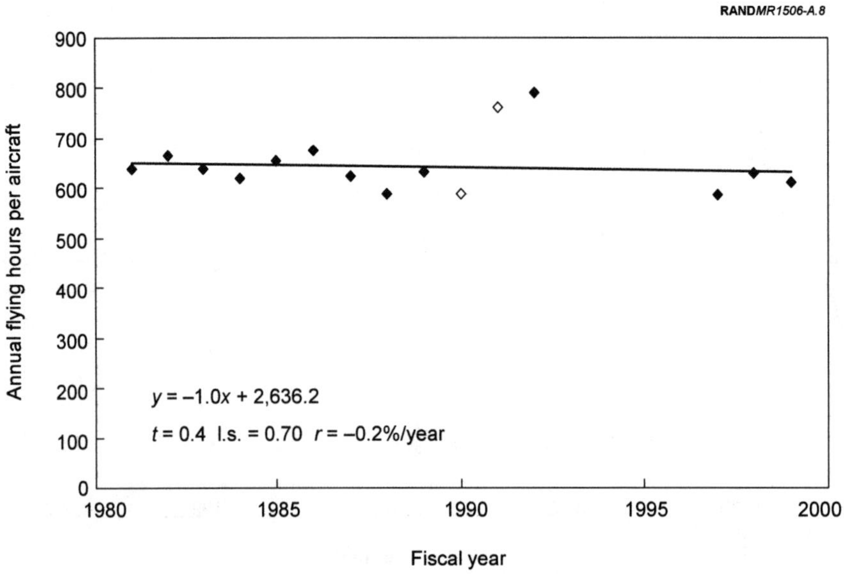

NOTE: Data points for 1990 and 1991 were excluded from the determination of the trend line.

Figure A.8—C-130 Annual Flying Hours per Aircraft During Peacetime

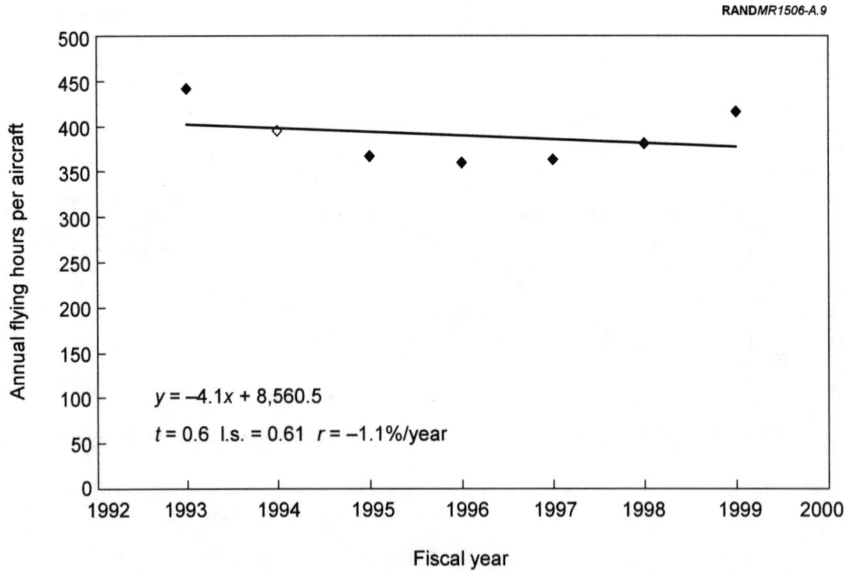

NOTE: The data point for 1994 was excluded from the determination of the trend line.

Figure A.9—KC-135 Annual Flying Hours per Aircraft During Peacetime

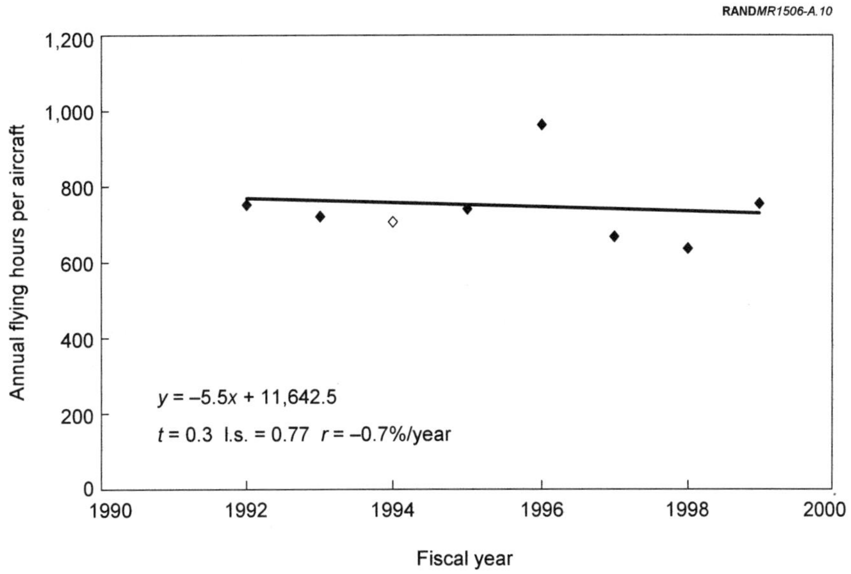

NOTE: The data point for 1994 was excluded from the determination of the trend line.

Figure A.10—KC-10 Annual Flying Hours per Aircraft During Peacetime

Also, the large number of flying hours per aircraft during FY 1992, as shown in Figure A.8, calls for an explanation. The total flying hours for C-130s during FY 1992 declined to 88,500 hours from the Gulf War level of 146,000 hours during FY 1991. On the other hand, the number of C-130s under AMC declined from 246 in FY 1981 to 192 in FY 1991, or 22 percent over the decade. Yet the number dropped sharply to 112 during FY 1992, representing a 42 percent decline in a single year. When C-130s were transferred back to AMC in FY 1997, the number was further reduced to 84, where it remained throughout FY 1998 and FY 1999. The much sharper drop in the number of C-130s than in flying hours caused the annual flying hours per aircraft to rise to 790 (i.e., 88,500/112) in FY 1992, as compared to 762 in FY 1991.

KC-135 and KC-10 tankers have been under the control of AMC since FY 1992. They were previously under the Strategic Air Command. Throughout the report, we do not use data prior to FY 1992 in tanker figures because data under different commands may not be comparable.

The sharply higher value in KC-10s for FY 1996 (Figure A.10) was caused mainly by the resumption of attacks on Bosnian-Serb military targets under the provisions of Operation Deliberate Force, the humanitarian airlift (Operation Provide Promise) and peacekeeping mission in Bosnia, and air refuelings of B-52s for the military strike on Iraq in Operation Desert Strike.

MONTHLY FLYING HOURS PER COPILOT

Figures A.11 to A.15, along with Figure 2.7 for the C-5 in the text, form a set of graphs showing monthly flying hours per CP for the six organic aircraft.

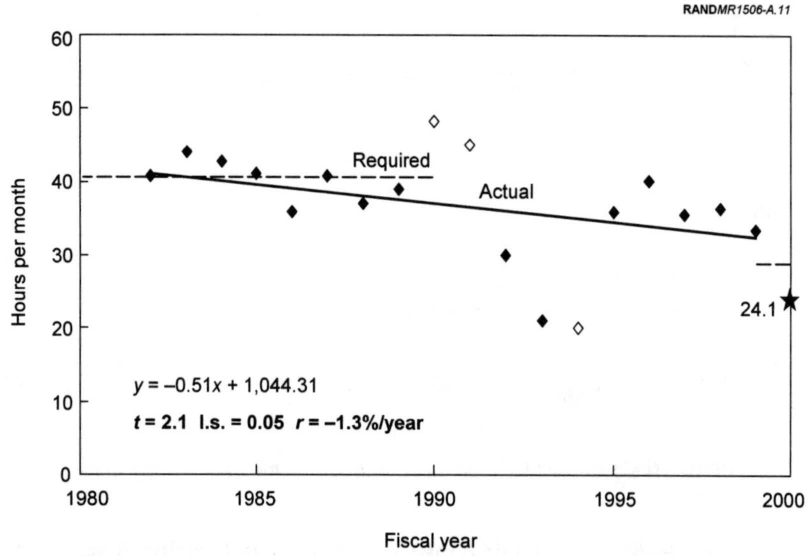

NOTE: Data points for 1990, 1991, 1994, and 2000 were excluded from the determination of the trend line.

Figure A.11—C-141 Monthly Flying Hours per Copilot

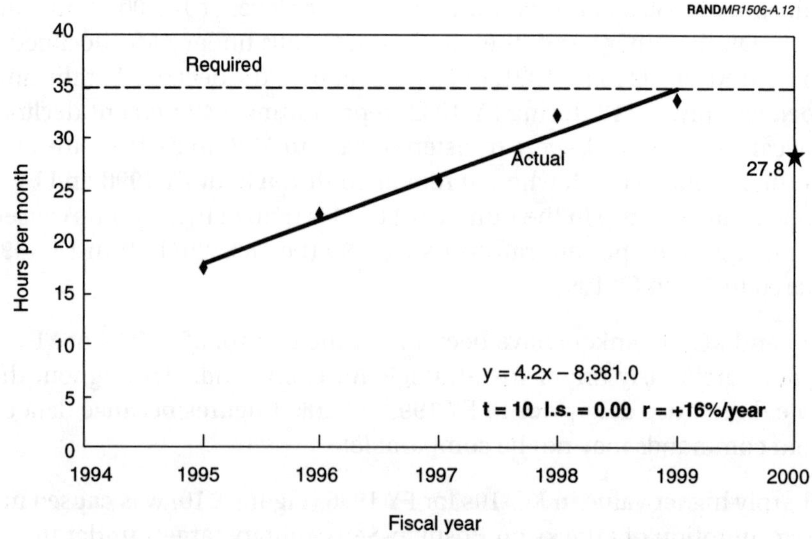

NOTE: The data point for 2000 was excluded from the determination of the trend line.

Figure A.12—C-17 Monthly Flying Hours per Copilot

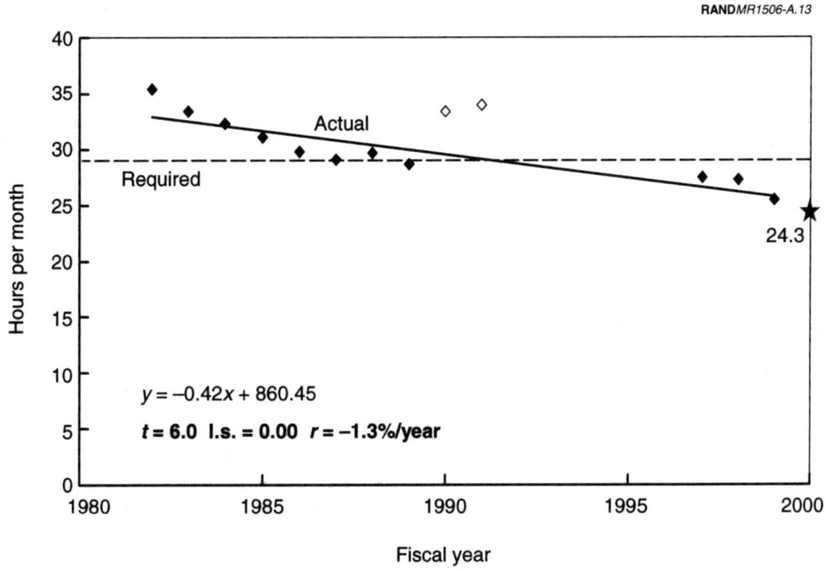

NOTE: Data points for 1990, 1991, and 2000 were excluded from the determination of the trend line.

Figure A.13—C-130 Monthly Flying Hours per Copilot

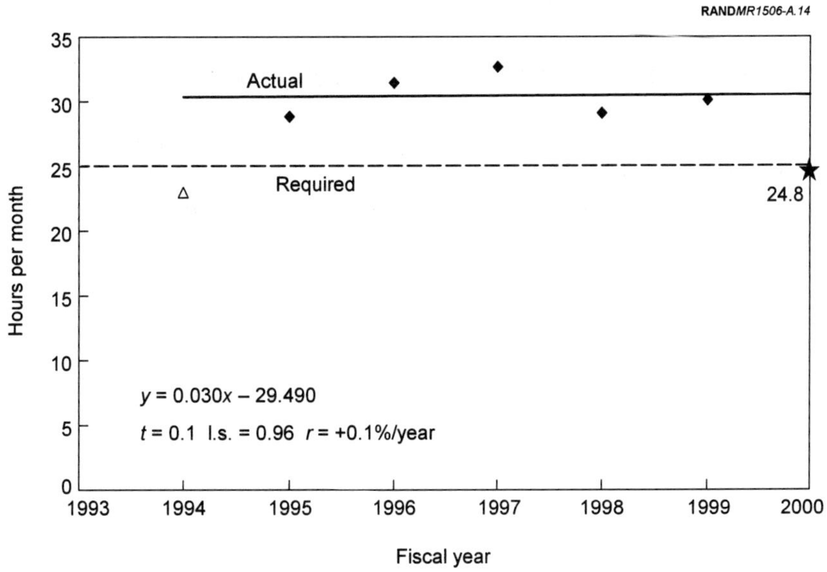

NOTE: Data points for 1994 and 2000 were excluded from the determination of the trend line.

Figure A.14—KC-135 Monthly Flying Hours per Copilot

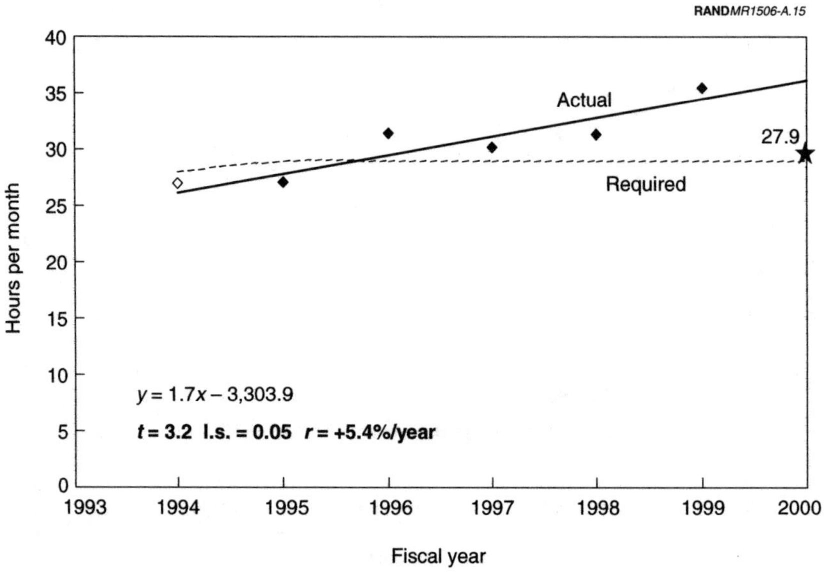

NOTE: Data points for 1994 and 2000 were excluded from the determination of the trend line.

Figure A.15—KC-10 Monthly Flying Hours per Copilot

MONTHLY FLYING HOURS PER AIRCRAFT COMMANDER

Figures A.16 to A.21 show the monthly flying hours per AC discussed in Chapter Two. For ease of comparison with CP flying hours, we leave the line indicating the CPs' aging requirement in these AC graphs even though ACs do not have to meet this requirement.

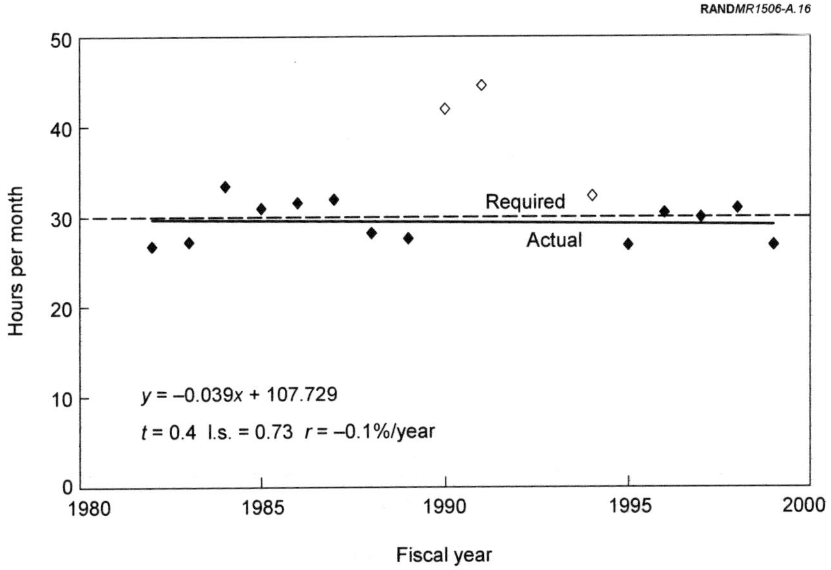

NOTE: Data points for 1990, 1991, and 1994 were excluded from the determination of the trend line.

Figure A.16—C-5 Monthly Flying Hours per Aircraft Commander

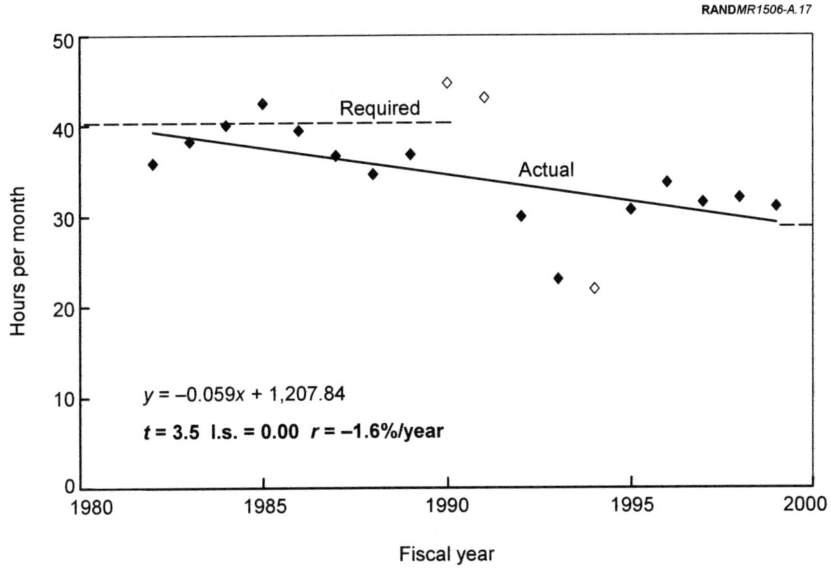

NOTE: Data points for 1990, 1991, and 1994 were excluded from the determination of the trend line.

Figure A.17—C-141 Monthly Flying Hours per Aircraft Commander

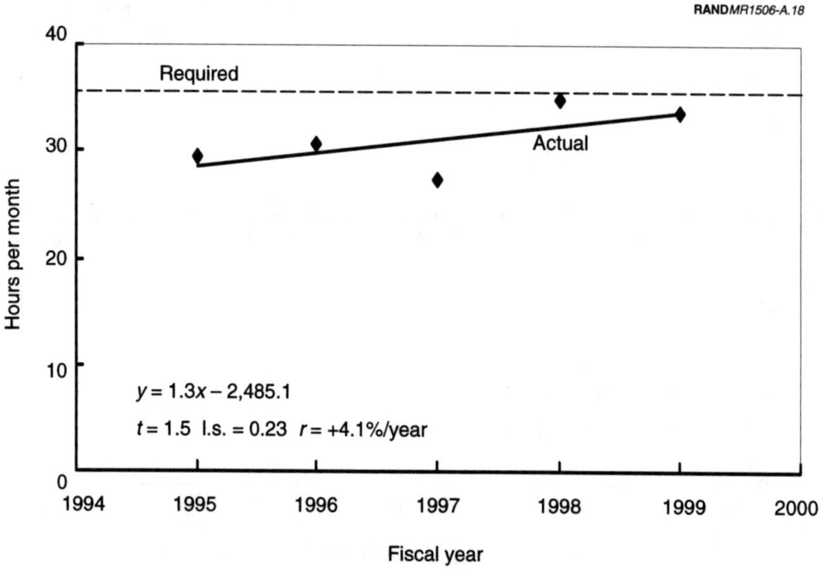

Figure A.18—C-17 Monthly Flying Hours per Aircraft Commander

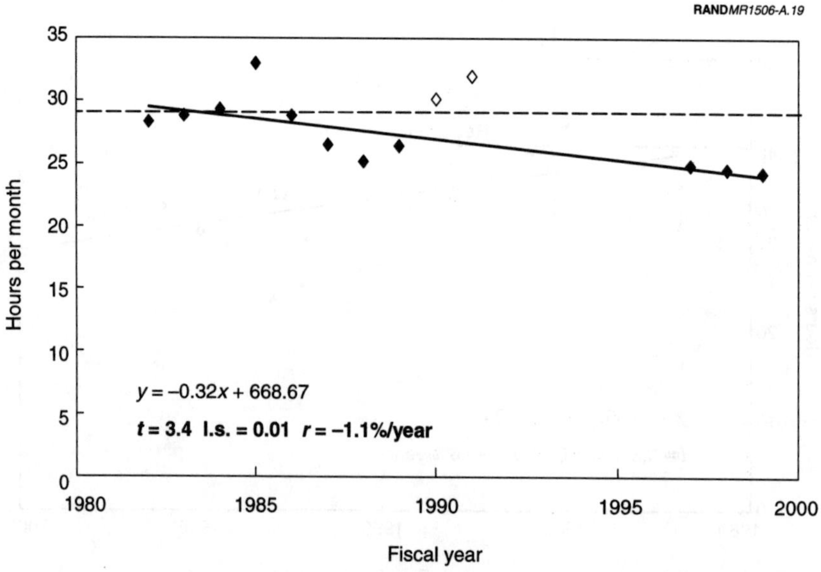

Figure A.19—C-130 Monthly Flying Hours per Aircraft Commander

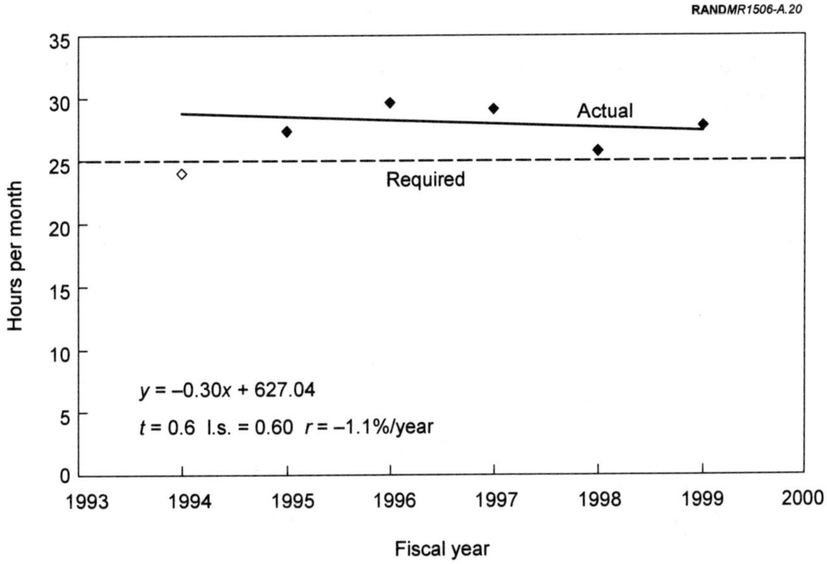

NOTE: The data point for 1994 was excluded from the determination of the trend line.

Figure A.20—KC-135 Monthly Flying Hours per Aircraft Commander

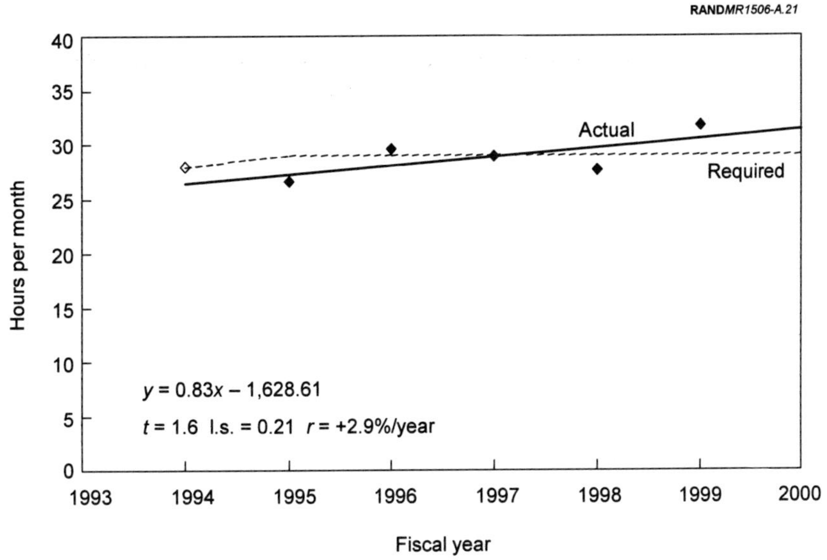

NOTE: The data point for 1994 was excluded from the determination of the trend line.

Figure A.21—KC-10 Monthly Flying Hours per Aircraft Commander

CHANNEL, ENGAGEMENT, AND O&M FLYING

Figure A.22 shows that channel flying declined the fastest in the 1990s, as discussed in Chapter Two.

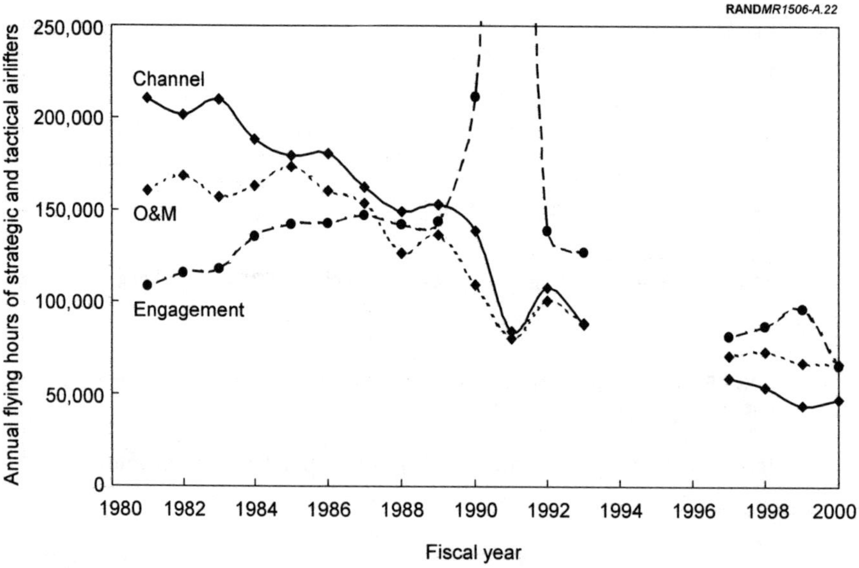

Figure A.22—Channel Flying Declined Faster than Engagement and O&M over the Past Two Decades

ANNUAL FLYING HOURS IN THREE MISSION CATEGORIES

Along with Figure 2.12 for the C-5, Figures A.23 to A.25 form a set of airlifter graphs for annual flying hours in three mission categories.

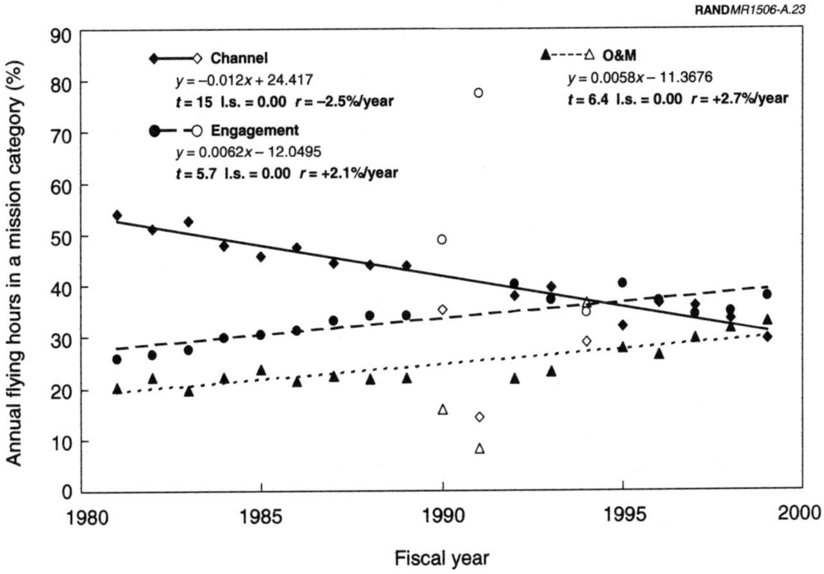

NOTE: Data points for 1990, 1991, and 1994 were excluded from the determination of the trend lines.

Figure A.23—C-141: Growing Engagement Missions and Declining Channel Missions

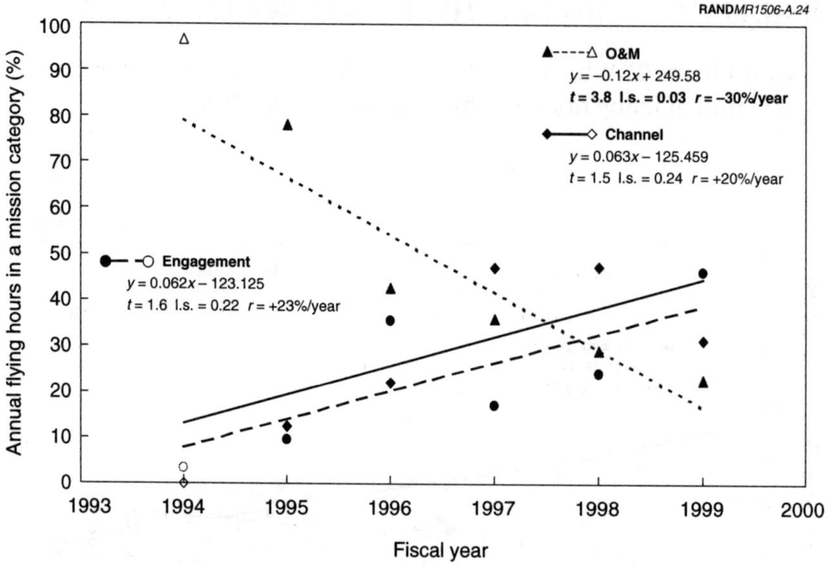

NOTE: Data points for 1994 were excluded from the determination of the trend lines.

Figure A.24—C-17: Percentages of Annual Flying Hours in Three Mission Categories

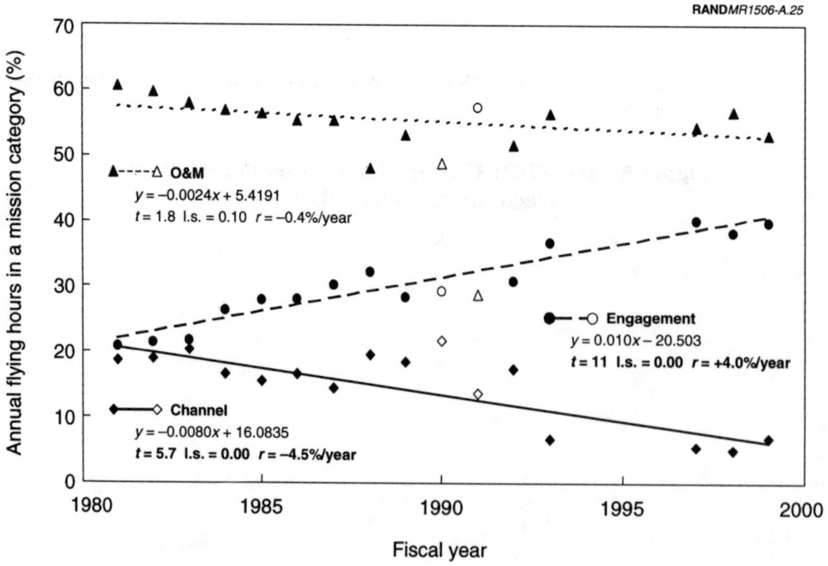

NOTE: Data points for 1990 and 1991 were excluded from the determination of the trend lines.

Figure A.25—C-130: Growing Engagement Missions and Declining Channel Missions

ACTUAL AND AUTHORIZED CP/AC RATIOS

Figures A.26 to A.30, along with Figure 3.2 in the text for the C-5, constitute a set of graphs for actual and authorized CP/AC ratios.

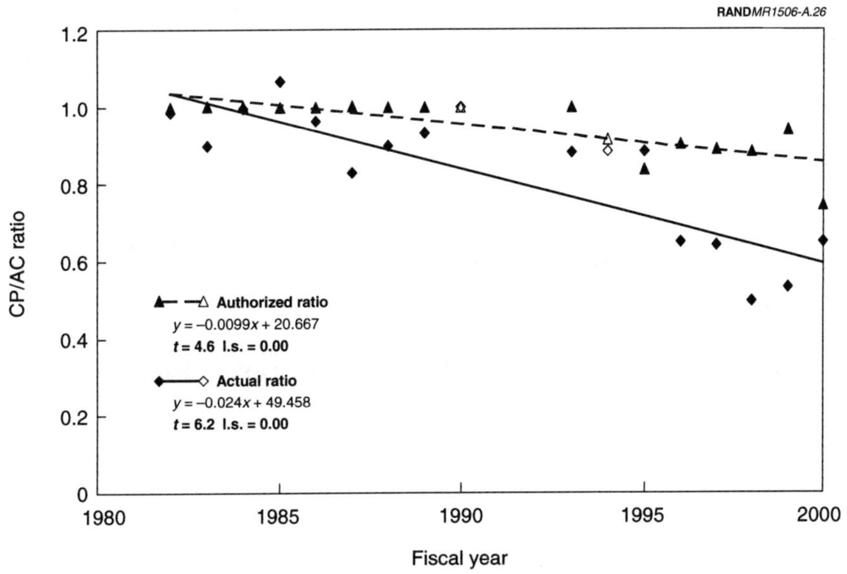

NOTE: Data points for 1990 and 1994 were excluded from the determination of the trend lines.

Figure A.26—C-141: Actual and Authorized CP/AC Ratios

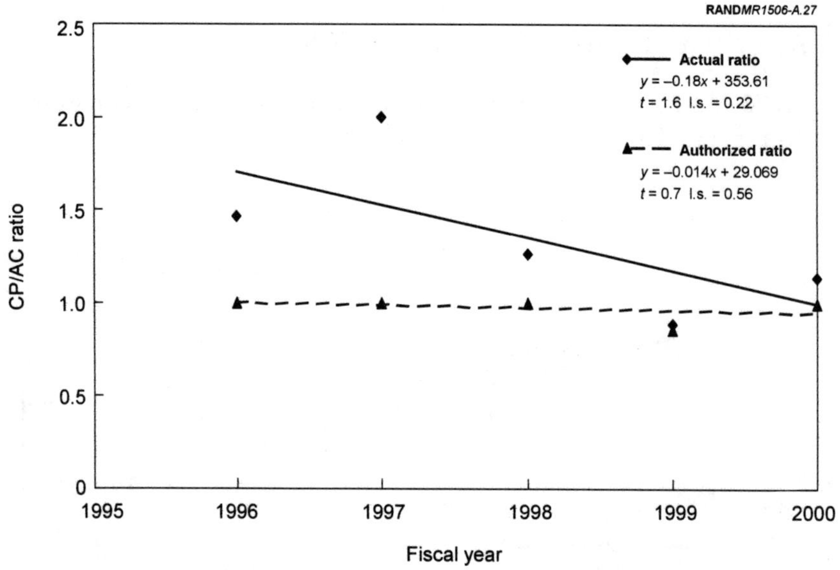

Figure A.27—C-17: Actual and Authorized CP/AC Ratios

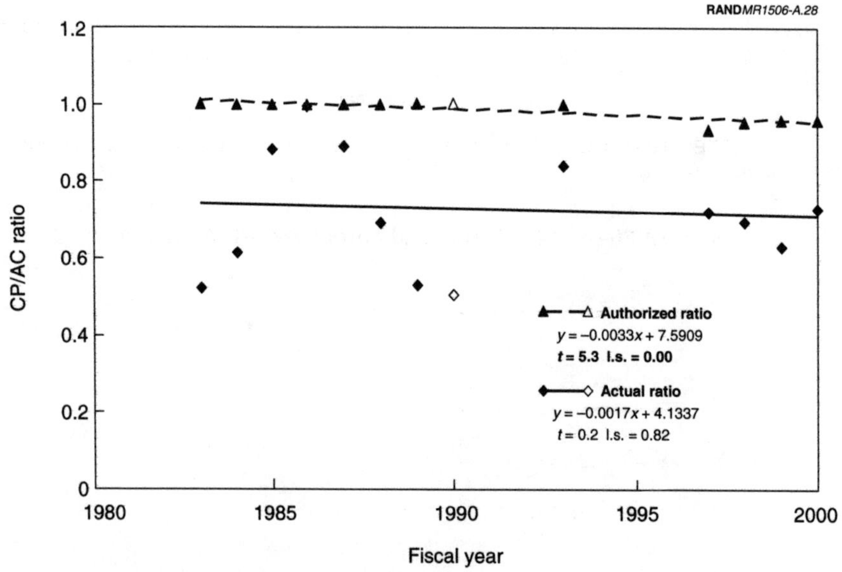

NOTE: Data points for 1990 were excluded from the determination of the trend lines.

Figure A.28—C-130: Actual and Authorized CP/AC Ratios

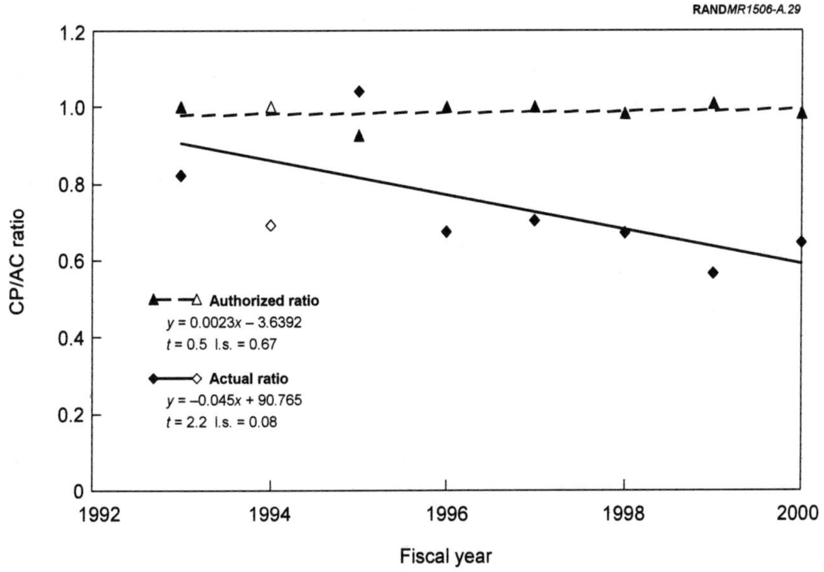

NOTE: Data points for 1994 were excluded from the determination of the trend lines.

Figure A.29—KC-135: Actual and Authorized CP/AC Ratios

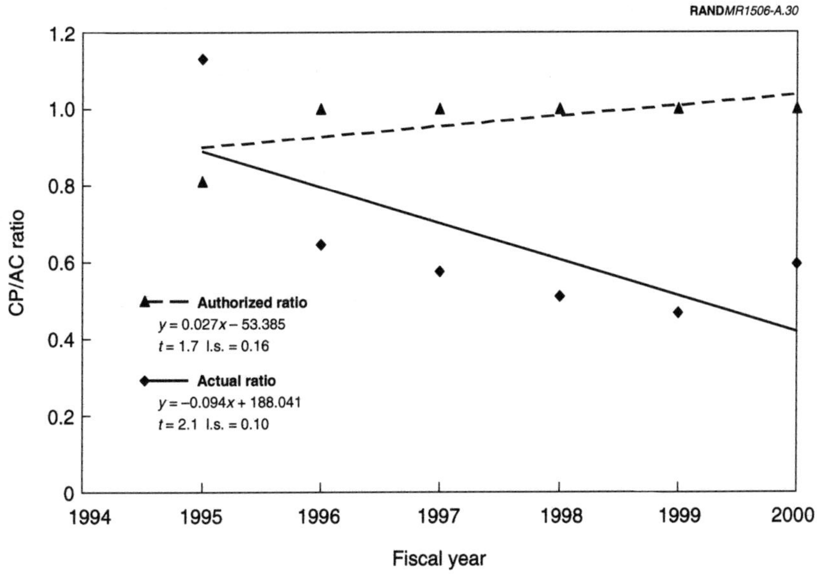

Figure A.30—KC-10: Actual and Authorized CP/AC Ratios

ACTUAL AND PROGRAMMED ANNUAL FLYING HOURS

Figure 5.1 for the C-5 and Figures A.31 to A.35 are a set of graphs for the six organic assets showing their actual and programmed annual flying hours.

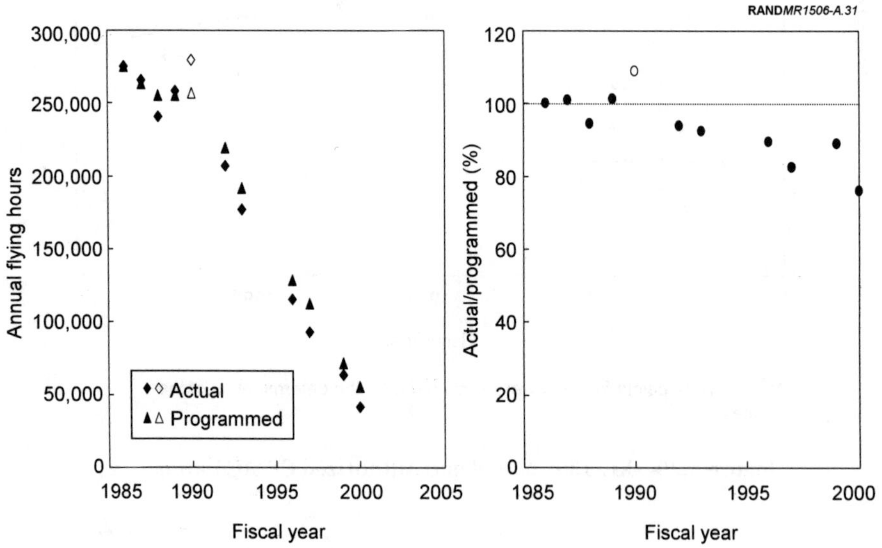

Figure A.31—C-141 Annual Flying Hours

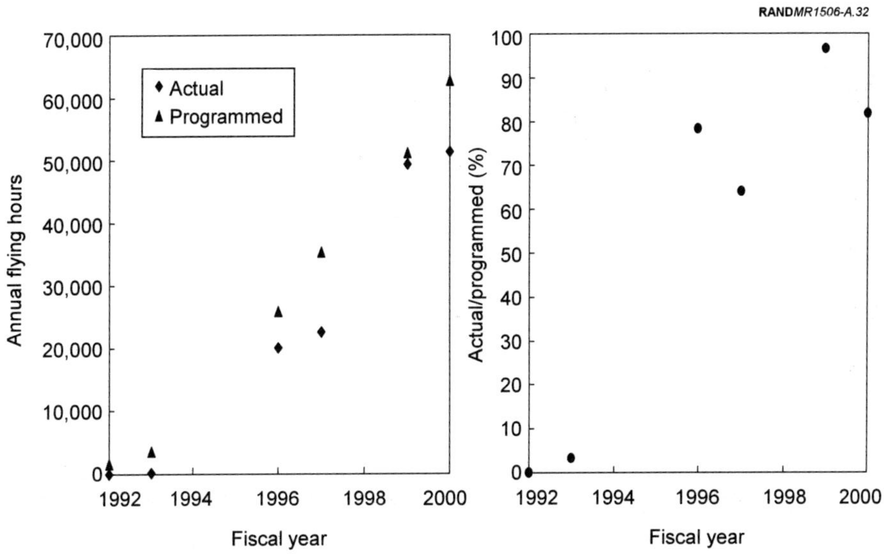

Figure A.32—C-17 Annual Flying Hours

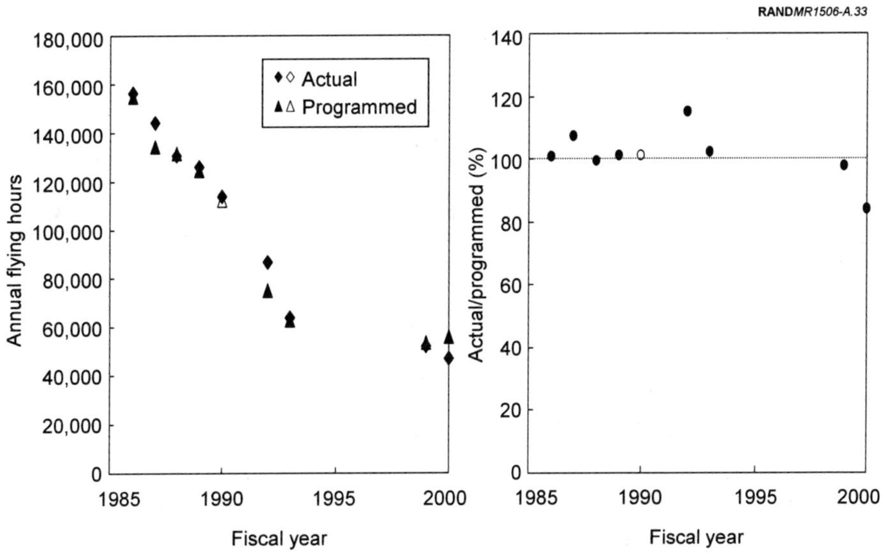

Figure A.33—C-130 Annual Flying Hours

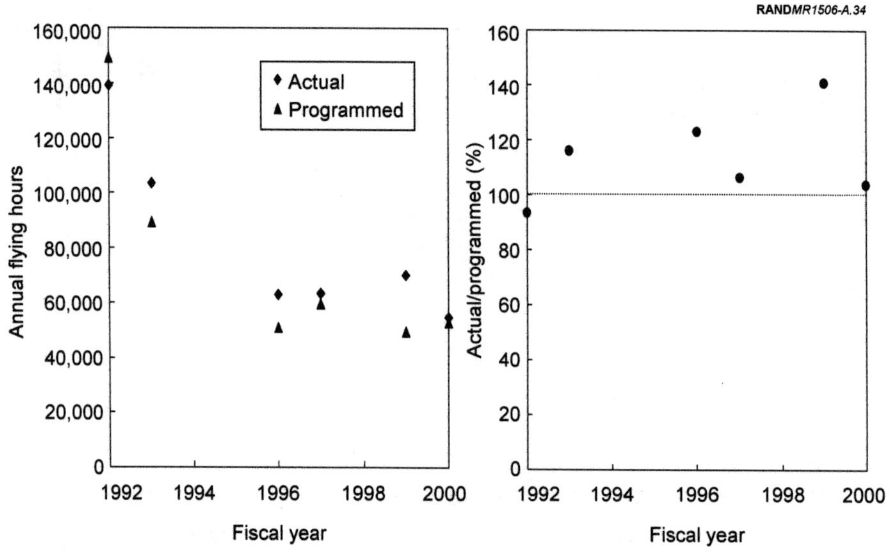

Figure A.34—KC-135 Annual Flying Hours

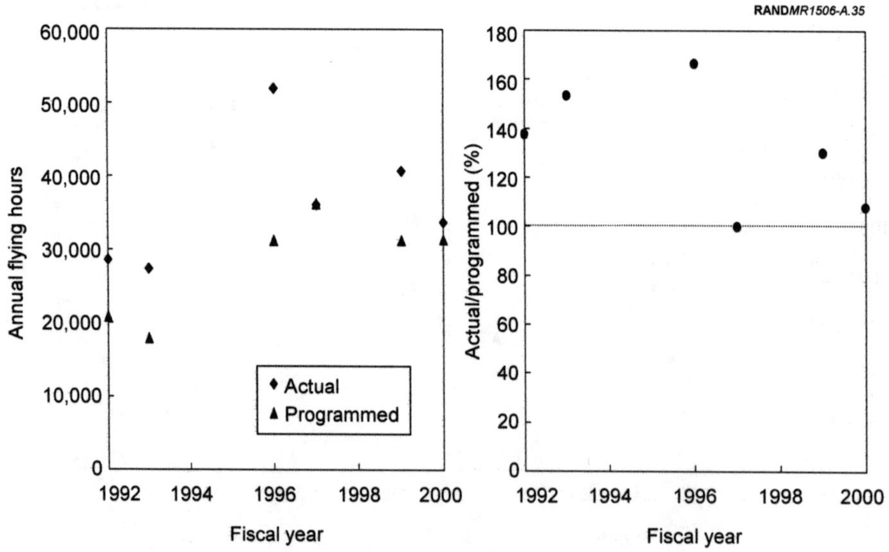

Figure A.35—KC-10 Annual Flying Hours

FLYING HOUR DEVIATION FROM PLANNED

Figures A.36 to A.38 are the graphs associated with Figure 5.4, showing the flying hour deviation from planned for the four airlifters.

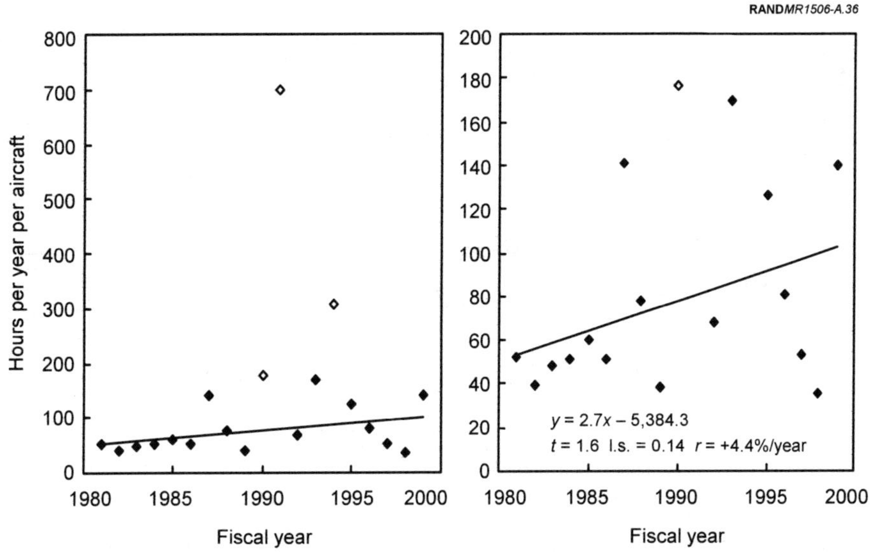

NOTE: Data points for 1990, 1991, and 1994 were excluded from the determination of the trend lines.

Figure A.36—C-141 Flying-Hour Deviation from Planned

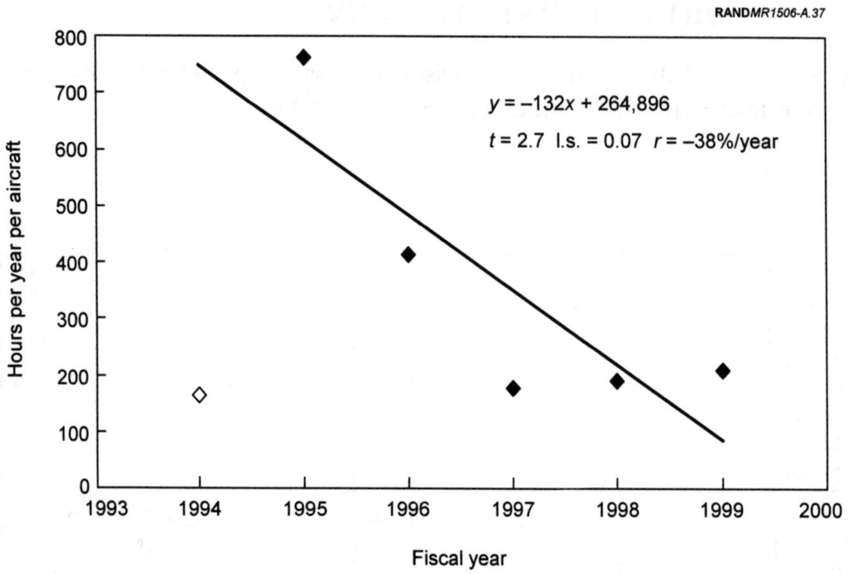

NOTE: The data point for 1994 was excluded from the determination of the trend line.

Figure A.37—C-17 Flying-Hour Deviation from Planned

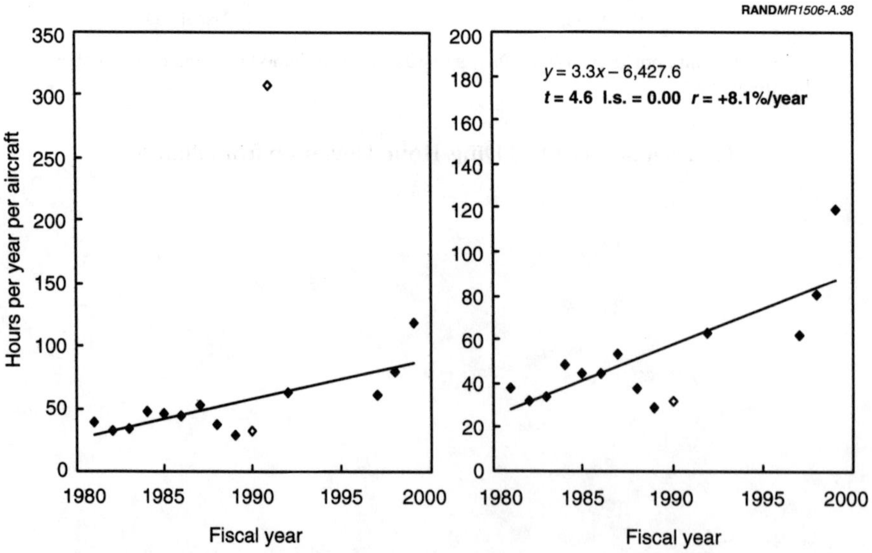

NOTE: Data points for 1990 and 1991 were excluded from the determination of the trend lines.

Figure A.38—C-130 Flying-Hour Deviation from Planned

PEAK GREATER-THAN-PLANNED FLYING HOURS PER AIRCRAFT

Figures A.39 to A.42 show the peak GTP flying hours per aircraft for the airlifters, as was discussed in Chapter Five.

RANDMR1506-A.39

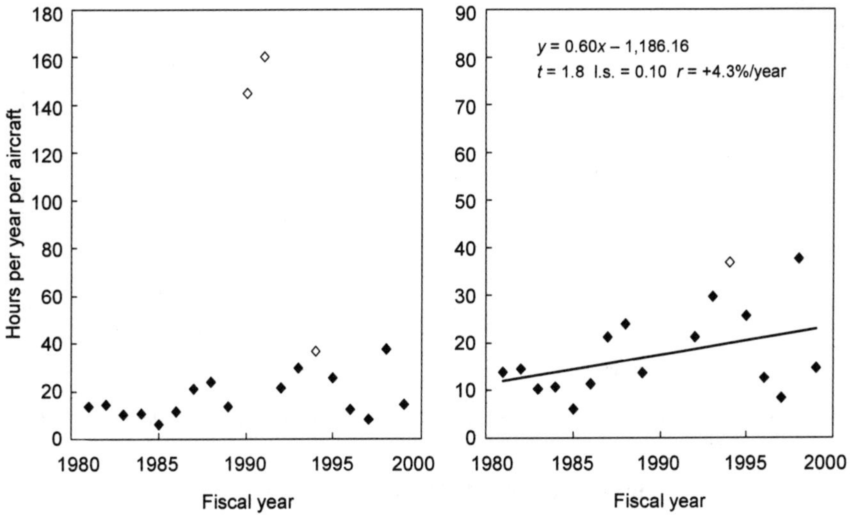

NOTE: Data points for 1990, 1991, and 1994 were excluded from the determination of the trend line.

Figure A.39—C-5 Peak GTP Flying Hours

RANDMR1506-A.40

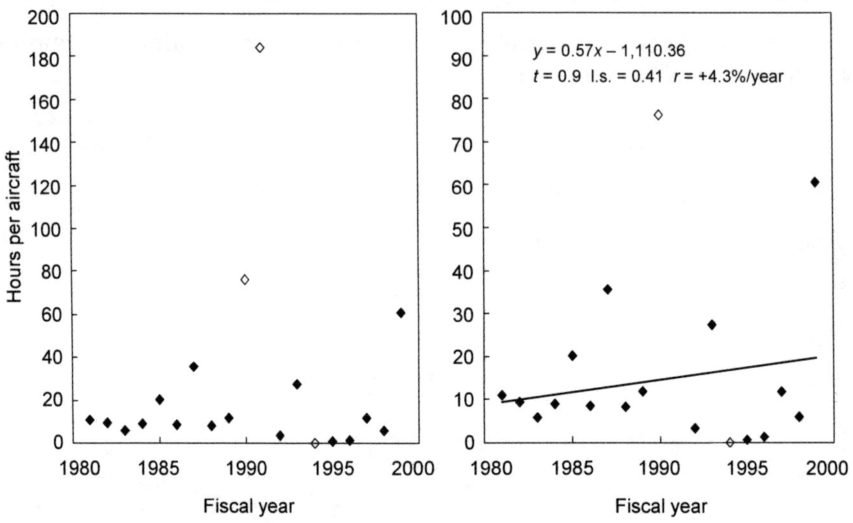

NOTE: Data points for 1990, 1991, and 1994 were excluded from the determination of the trend line.

Figure A.40—C-141 Peak GTP Flying Hours

RANDMR1506-A.41

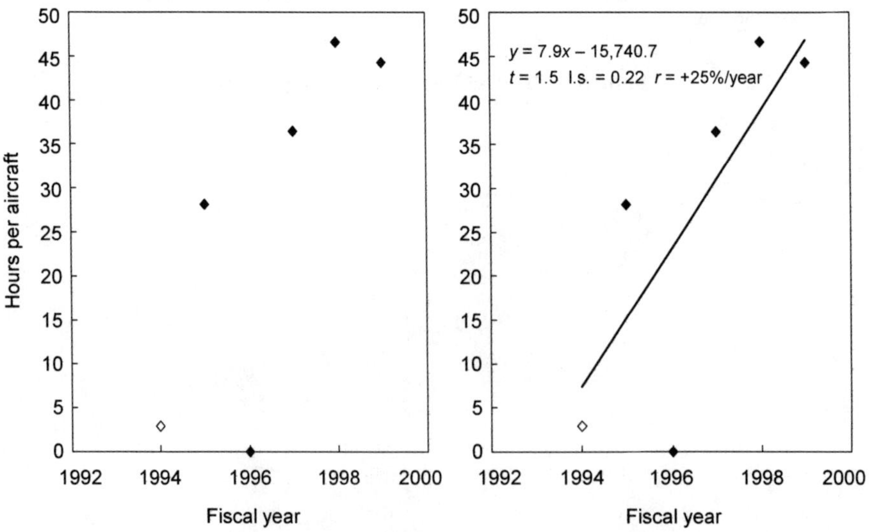

NOTE: The data point for 1994 was excluded from the determination of the trend lines.

Figure A.41—C-17 Peak GTP Flying Hours

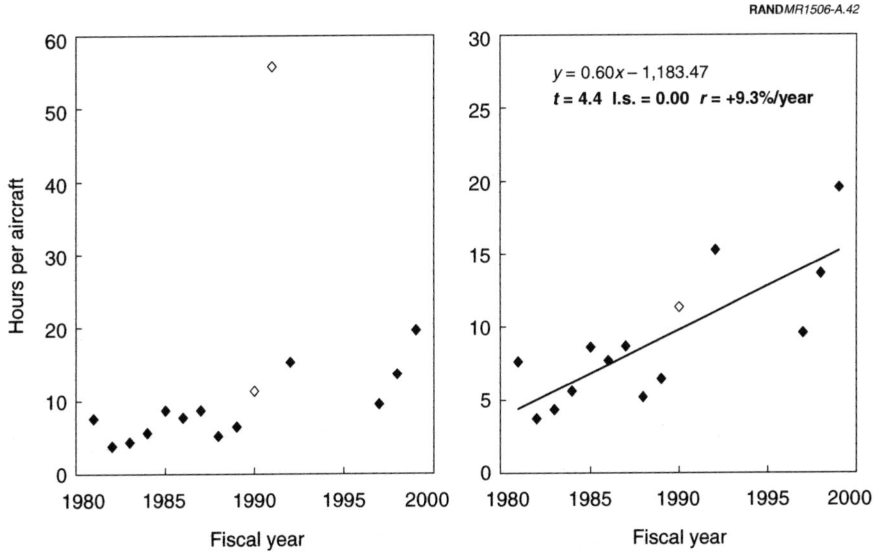

NOTE: Data points for 1990 and 1991 were excluded from the determination of the trend line.

Figure A.42—C-130 Peak GTP Flying Hours

LENGTH OF GREATER-THAN-PLANNED FLYING

Figures A.43 to A.46 show the length of uninterrupted monthly GTP flying hours for the airlifters, as was discussed in Chapter Five.

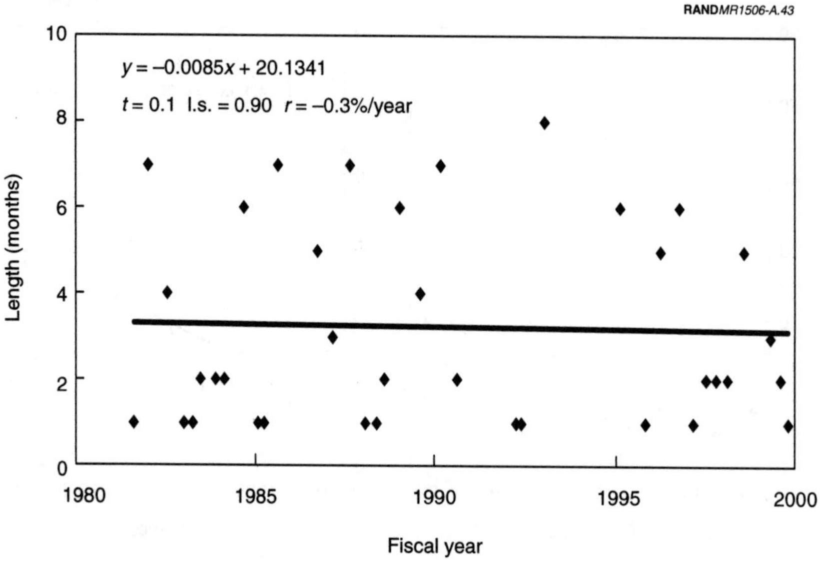

NOTE: Excludes periods related to Gulf War and C-141 repair.

Figure A.43—C-5 Length of Uninterrupted Monthly GTP Flying Hours

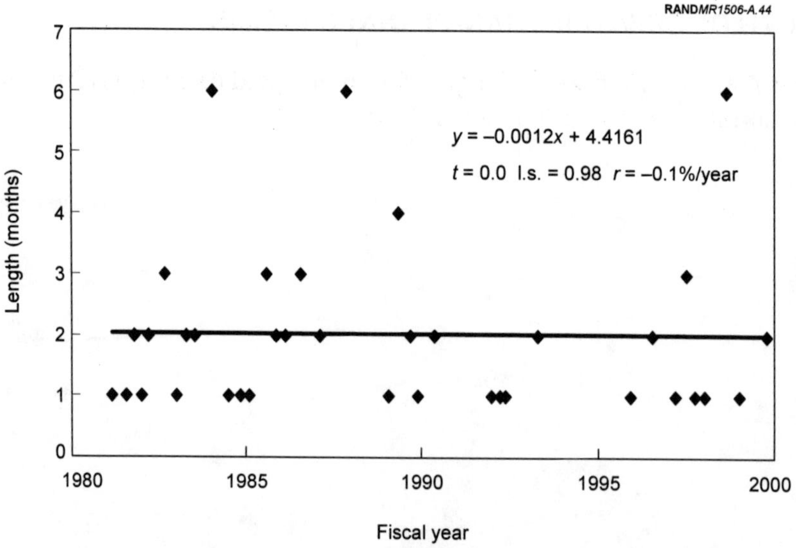

NOTE: Excludes periods related to Gulf War and C-141 repair.

Figure A.44—C-141 Length of Uninterrupted Monthly GTP Flying Hours

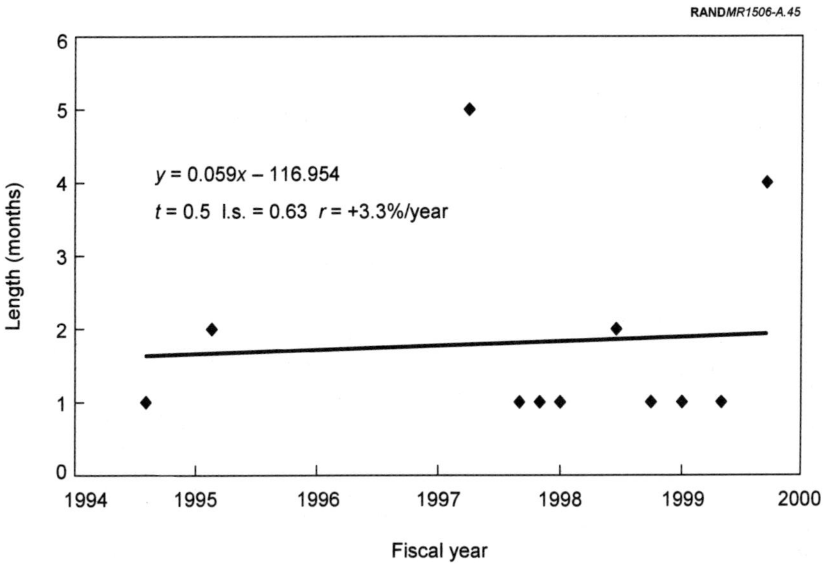

NOTE: Excludes periods related to C-141 repair.

Figure A.45—C-17 Length of Uninterrupted Monthly GTP Flying Hours

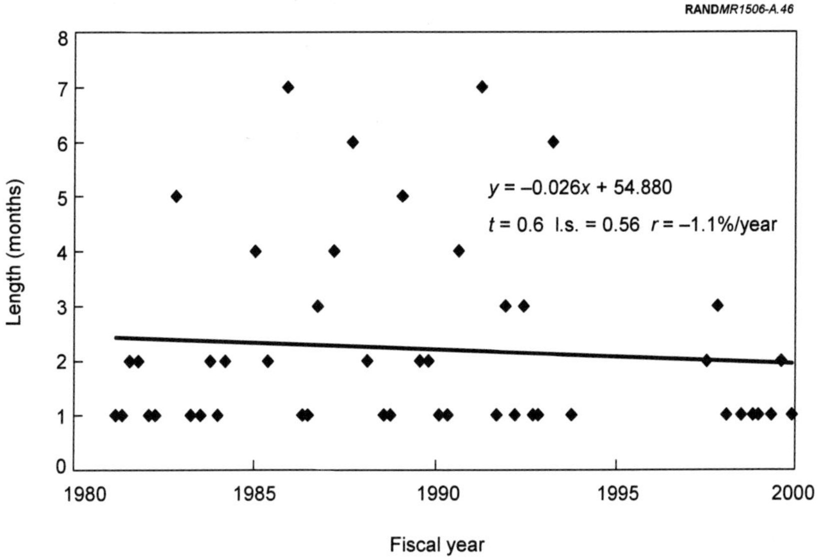

NOTE: Excludes periods related to Gulf War and C-141 repair.

Figure A.46—C-130 Length of Uninterrupted Monthly GTP Flying Hours

AMC BUDGET

Figure A.47 shows the AMC budget in three components: military O&M, commercial TWCF, and military TWCF, as discussed in Chapter Six.

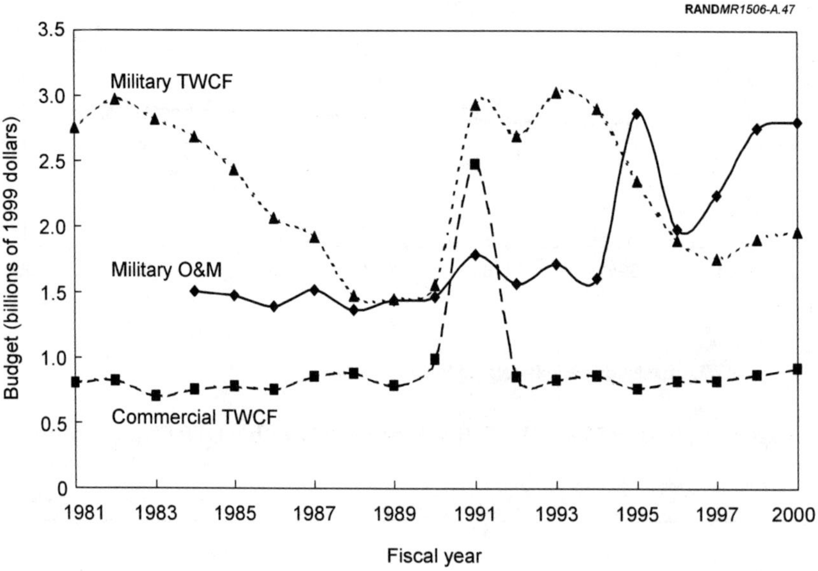

Figure A.47—AMC TWCF and O&M Budget

COMMERCIAL AUGMENTATION

Figures A.48 through A.50 show the commercial share of channel cargo in dollars, channel passengers in passenger-miles, and channel cargo in ton-miles, as discussed in Chapter Six.

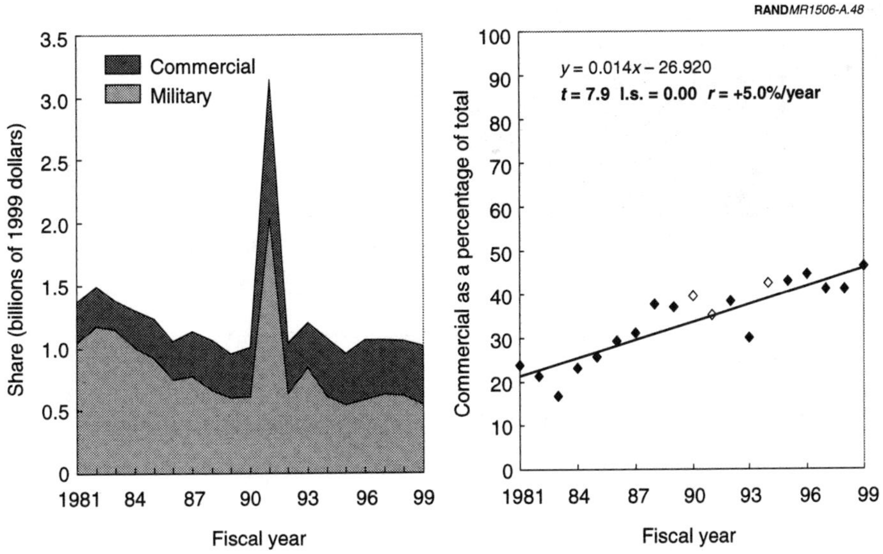

NOTE: Data points for 1990, 1991, and 1994 were excluded from the trend line.

Figure A.48—Commercial Carriers' Share of Channel Cargo Is Increasing

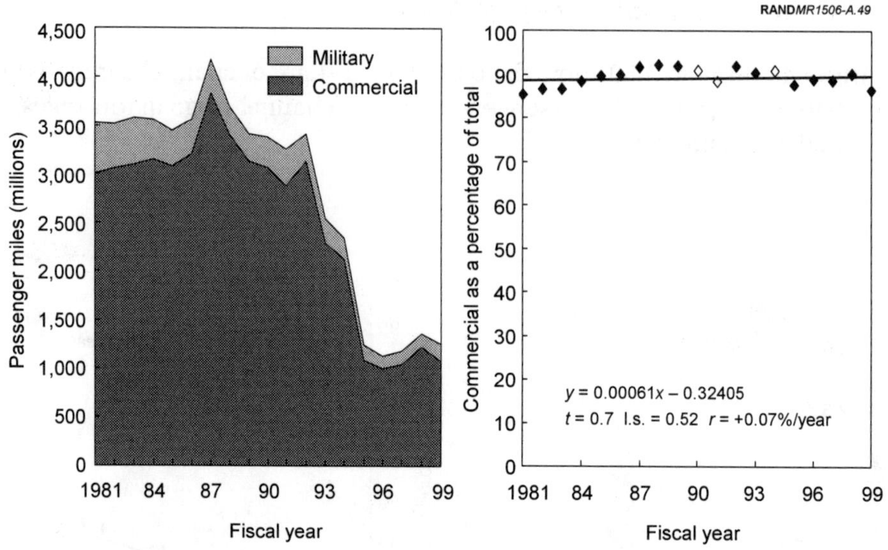

NOTE: Data points for 1990, 1991, and 1994 were excluded from the determination of the trend line.

Figure A.49—Commercial Augmentation Has Continued to Dominate Channel Passenger Miles

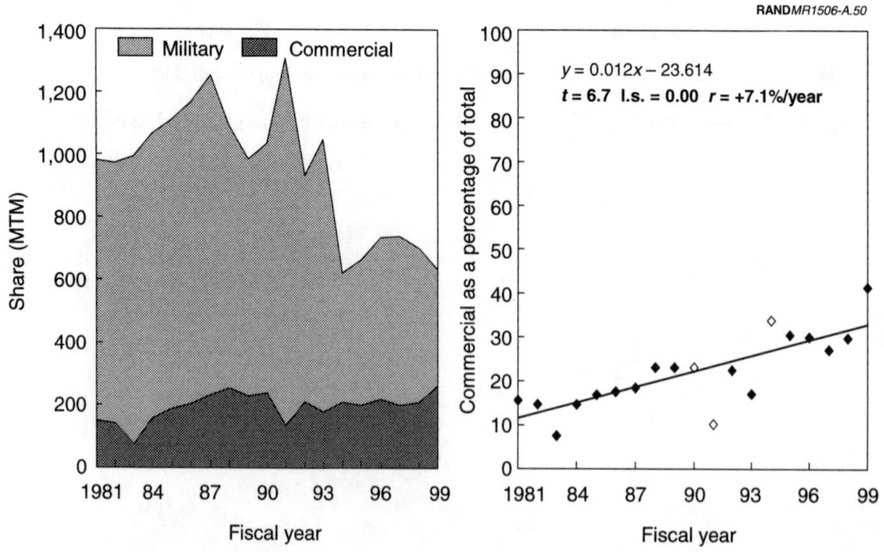

NOTE: Data points for 1990, 1991, and 1994 were excluded from the determination of the trend line.

Figure A.50—Increasing Share of Commercial Augmentation in Ton-Miles for Channel Cargo